Interracial America

Opposing Viewpoints®

Interracial America

Opposing Viewpoints®

Other Books of Related Interest

Interracial America

Opposing Viewpoints®

Eleanor Stanford, *Book Editor*

Bonnie Szumski, *Publisher*
Helen Cothran, *Managing Editor*

OPPOSING
VIEWPOINTS®
SERIES

GREENHAVEN PRESS
An imprint of Thomson Gale, a part of The Thomson Corporation

THOMSON
™
GALE

Detroit • New York • San Francisco • San Diego • New Haven, Conn.
Waterville, Maine • London • Munich

© 2006 Thomson Gale, a part of The Thomson Corporation.

Thomson and Star Logo are trademarks and Gale and Greenhaven Press are registered trademarks used herein under license.

For more information, contact
Greenhaven Press
27500 Drake Rd.
Farmington Hills, MI 48331-3535
Or you can visit our Internet site at http://www.gale.com

Greenhaven Press anthologies primarily consist of previously published material taken from a variety of sources, including periodicals, books, scholarly journals, newspapers, government documents, and position papers from private and public organizations. These original sources are often edited for length and to ensure their accessibility for a young adult audience. The anthology editors also change the original titles of these works in order to clearly present the main thesis of each viewpoint and to explicitly indicate the opinion presented in the viewpoint. These alterations are made in consideration of both the reading and comprehension levels of a young adult audience. Every effort is made to ensure that Greenhaven Press accurately reflects the original intent of the authors included in this anthology.

LIBRARY OF CONGRESS CATALOGING-IN-PUBLICATION DATA

Interracial America : opposing viewpoints / Eleanor Stanford, book editor.
    p. cm. — (Opposing viewpoints series)
Includes bibliographical references and index.
ISBN 0-7377-2943-0 (lib. : alk. paper) — ISBN 0-7377-2944-9 (pbk. : alk. paper)
    1. United States—Race relations. 2. United States—Ethnic relations.
3. Ethnicity—United States. I. Stanford, Eleanor. II. Opposing viewpoints series (Unnumbered)
E184.A1I593 2006
305.800973—dc22
                                                    2005054893

Printed in the United States of America

"Congress shall make no law. . . abridging the freedom of speech, or of the press."

First Amendment to the U.S. Constitution

The basic foundation of our democracy is the First Amendment guarantee of freedom of expression. The Opposing Viewpoints Series is dedicated to the concept of this basic freedom and the idea that it is more important to practice it than to enshrine it.

Contents

Why Consider Opposing Viewpoints?

"The only way in which a human being can make some approach to knowing the whole of a subject is by hearing what can be said about it by persons of every variety of opinion and studying all modes in which it can be looked at by every character of mind. No wise man ever acquired his wisdom in any mode but this."

John Stuart Mill

In our media-intensive culture it is not difficult to find differing opinions. Thousands of newspapers and magazines and dozens of radio and television talk shows resound with differing points of view. The difficulty lies in deciding which opinion to agree with and which "experts" seem the most credible. The more inundated we become with differing opinions and claims, the more essential it is to hone critical reading and thinking skills to evaluate these ideas. Opposing Viewpoints books address this problem directly by presenting stimulating debates that can be used to enhance and teach these skills. The varied opinions contained in each book examine many different aspects of a single issue. While examining these conveniently edited opposing views, readers can develop critical thinking skills such as the ability to compare and contrast authors' credibility, facts, argumentation styles, use of persuasive techniques, and other stylistic tools. In short, the Opposing Viewpoints Series is an ideal way to attain the higher-level thinking and reading skills so essential in a culture of diverse and contradictory opinions.

In addition to providing a tool for critical thinking, Opposing Viewpoints books challenge readers to question their own strongly held opinions and assumptions. Most people form their opinions on the basis of upbringing, peer pressure, and personal, cultural, or professional bias. By reading carefully balanced opposing views, readers must directly confront new ideas as well as the opinions of those with whom they disagree. This is not to simplistically argue that everyone who reads opposing views will—or should—change his or her opinion. Instead, the series enhances readers' understanding of their own views by encouraging confrontation with opposing ideas. Careful examination of others' views can lead to the readers' understanding of the logical inconsistencies in their own opinions, perspective on why they hold an opinion, and the consideration of the possibility that their opinion requires further evaluation.

Evaluating Other Opinions

To ensure that this type of examination occurs, Opposing Viewpoints books present all types of opinions. Prominent spokespeople on different sides of each issue as well as well-known professionals from many disciplines challenge the reader. An additional goal of the series is to provide a forum for other, less known, or even unpopular viewpoints. The opinion of an ordinary person who has had to make the decision to cut off life support from a terminally ill relative, for example, may be just as valuable and provide just as much insight as a medical ethicist's professional opinion. The editors have two additional purposes in including these less known views. One, the editors encourage readers to respect others' opinions—even when not enhanced by professional credibility. It is only by reading or listening to and objectively evaluating others' ideas that one can determine whether they are worthy of consideration. Two, the inclusion of such viewpoints encourages the important critical thinking skill of objectively evaluating an author's credentials and bias. This evaluation will illuminate an author's reasons for taking a particular stance on an issue and will aid in readers' evaluation of the author's ideas.

It is our hope that these books will give readers a deeper understanding of the issues debated and an appreciation of the complexity of even seemingly simple issues when good and honest people disagree. This awareness is particularly important in a democratic society such as ours in which people enter into public debate to determine the common good. Those with whom one disagrees should not be regarded as enemies but rather as people whose views deserve careful examination and may shed light on one's own.

Thomas Jefferson once said that "difference of opinion leads to inquiry, and inquiry to truth." Jefferson, a broadly educated man, argued that "if a nation expects to be ignorant and free . . . it expects what never was and never will be." As individuals and as a nation, it is imperative that we consider the opinions of others and examine them with skill and discernment. The Opposing Viewpoints Series is intended to help readers achieve this goal.

David L. Bender and Bruno Leone,
Founders

Introduction

"Hurricane Katrina survivors didn't have the cars, the gas, the locations where they could relocate to. . . . But that's true in every day life also. Poor people, disproportionately African-Americans, Hispanics, Asian-Americans . . . have little capacity to get away from bad things."
—*Congressman Melvin L. Watt (Democrat-N.C.)*

Rooftops protruded from six feet of murky water. Helicopters whirred down from the sky to pull stranded residents from their attics. In a football stadium thousands huddled on cots. Evacuees who had made it to dry land built makeshift shelters out of cardboard boxes, protecting themselves from the sun while they wondered how they would get drinking water or feed their children.

When Hurricane Katrina hit New Orleans, Louisiana, on August 29, 2005, the city, submerged in water, faced a crisis of enormous proportions. The breached levees would have to be rebuilt. Roads were washed out, dead bodies floated in the streets, and toxic sewage covered large swaths of the city. In television news coverage of the disaster, one thing was immediately and for many, shockingly obvious: Disproportionate numbers of those unable to evacuate and forced to fend for themselves in the submerged city were black. The tragedy has thrust the debate about race—and class—before the American people in a way that is difficult to ignore. Commentators debate whether race played a role in the fact that those who suffered the brunt of the disaster were largely black. They also ask whether race was a factor in delays in getting help to those who needed it. Some argue that Katrina exposed institutionalized racism in the United States, claiming that had a wealthy, primarily white area been hit, both preparation and response to the disaster would have been better. Others disagree, contending that racism was not a factor. In a time of crisis, they maintain, accusations of racism are misplaced and distract from rescue efforts. The country's racial divide regarding Katrina—some stressing the importance of race and others preferring to understate its importance—typifies debates about race in America.

Many analysts criticized the government's slow reaction time, contending that the inadequate response was due to racism. "I do think the nation would be responding differently if [the victims] were white elderly and white babies actually dying on the street and being covered with newspapers and shrouds and being left there," said David Billings of the People's Institute, a 25-year-old New Orleans–based organization focused on ending racism. Civil rights leader Jesse Jackson also sees the connection between the inadequate response to Katrina and a history of racism in America. "In this same city of New Orleans where slave ships landed, [a city with a] legacy of 246 years of slavery and 100 years of Jim Crow discrimination," Jackson maintains, "that legacy is unbroken today."

Others denied that there was any connection between the race of the victims and the government's slow response time. According to *National Review* writer Rich Lowry, "Sadly, poverty and age have affected who got out and who didn't, as many of the poor and elderly didn't have cars or the resources to evacuate. Many of these people are black, but . . . their skin color as such had nothing to do with whether they escaped the city." Some chose to understate or discount race as a factor in how help was meted out. Some even argued that the catastrophe would bring people of different races together, believing that a disaster such as Katrina would serve to unite people in an effort to help those who were suffering. Secretary of State Condoleeza Rice asserted, "that Americans would somehow, in a color-affected way, decide who to help and who not to help, I just don't believe it. Americans are generous to each other." At least in some instances, this appears to have been the case. Joseph Brant, a black man who said he escaped New Orleans by hitching a ride in a van carrying white people, said, "Before this whole thing, I had a complex about white people. This thing changed me forever."

Nevertheless, journalists and broadcasters, well aware that race is a sensitive issue in America and a risky topic for them to explore, soon found themselves having to mention the issue. On August 31, 2005, Jack Shafer, writing in *Slate* magazine, lamented the fact that "race remains largely untouchable for TV because broadcasters sense that they can't make an error without destroying careers." Whether because of articles like Shafer's or anger on the part of many victims, within several days of Shafer's article, the major networks had aired stories making explicit the connection between the race and poverty of the victims and their plight.

It remains to be seen whether the devastation caused by Hurricane Katrina will add fuel to debates about race in the United States or whether the issue will recede along with the floodwaters. The tragedy of Katrina has, however, proved to be a reminder of the fact that race remains an extremely sensitive issue in American society. The authors in *Opposing Viewpoints: Interracial America* explore the complexities of how race is experienced in America in the following chapters: Should America's Racial Differences Be Emphasized? What Impact Does Immigration Have on Interracial America? What Policies Promote Opportunities for All Races? How Should Society View Interracial Families? As Hurricane Katrina showed, charges of racism can ignite heated controversy, illustrating the challenges of living in an interracial society.

CHAPTER 1

Should America's Racial Differences Be Emphasized?

Chapter Preface

One of several debates in the controversy over whether racial differences should be emphasized concerns whether identifying racial differences will protect the health of those afflicted with race-specific diseases or will instead lead to discrimination. In recent years many in the scientific community have come to agree that race is a sociological rather than a biological construct. The Human Genome Project found that across races, human beings share 99.9 percent of the same genes. However, medical research often focuses more on racial differences than similarities. Racial predispositions to certain diseases have long been recognized. For example, sickle cell anemia is a disease that exists only among blacks, and the gene for the birth defect Tay-Sachs afflicts only Ashkenazi Jews. Some analysts argue that experiments using race-specific drugs are necessary to protect the health of those who are afflicted with such diseases. Others fear that such experiments could lead to discrimination.

Some researchers believe that experiments using race-specific drugs will save lives. The Food and Drug Administration (FDA) approved the first racially targeted drug, the heart failure medication called BiDil, in June 2005. During trials, the drug proved so effective in treating heart failure in blacks that the studies were ended early so those participants taking a placebo could be given the medication. FDA associate director of Medical Policy Robert Temple said, "The information presented to the FDA clearly showed that blacks suffering from heart failure will now have an additional safe and effective option for treating their condition."

While few would deny the legitimacy of medical advances that increase the treatment options of different groups, race-specific experiments make critics uneasy. Jonathan Kahn, a law professor at Hamline University, worries that BiDil's approval could be a step toward racial discrimination. "People look to this . . . and say, 'Look there really are differences between the races,'" he argues. "And in our country, historically, when you say races are different biologically, bad things happen," Kahn claims. Since research exploring racial difference has often been done in the service of racism, racially targeted research has been considered a taboo. The infamous Tuskegee syphilis experiment is an oft-cited example. The U.S. Public Heath Service, in an attempt to study the different ways syphilis affects blacks and whites, allowed 399 black men to go untreated, and in many cases, to remain unaware of their condition.

Some analysts argue that race-specific research is counterproductive. Francis Collins, the head of the National Human Genome Research Institute, asserts, "Research must move beyond these weak and imperfect proxy relationships [i.e., race] to define the more proximate factors that influence health." Opponents such as Collins claim that many of the racial differences being studied can often be accounted for by environmental factors such as access to healthy water, good nutrition, and medical insurance. A 2002 report by the Institute of Medicine showed that racial and ethnic minorities tend to receive lower-quality health care than whites, even accounting for such factors as insurance status, income, age, and severity of coalition. Critics of race-specific research contend all races would be best served by addressing these inequalities.

Whether race-specific drug experiments are beneficial or promote discrimination remains controversial. The authors in the following chapter debate other issues in the controversy over the benefits and detriments of emphasizing racial differences.

"Most everyone agrees that lines based on race—that is, systems of racial classification—are impermissible."

Racial Classifications Should Be Abandoned

Ward Connerly

In the following viewpoint Ward Connerly argues that racial classifications have historically been used to oppress African Americans. Without racial categories, he contends, slavery and segregation would have been impossible. Race is a social construct, not a biological reality, Connerly maintains. Doing away with racial categories, he claims, would allow Americans to define themselves as they choose and prevent the government from practicing racial discrimination. Connerly, chairman of the California Civil Rights Initiative campaign, is author of the book *Creating Equal*.

As you read, consider the following questions:

1. According to Connerly, in what way do U.S. laws rely on racial classification?
2. What is the impact of the "one drop" rule, in the author's view?
3. In the author's opinion, what different criteria are used to define race?

In a system of racial classification, government tracks the race of its population. In a system of racial discrimination, government, institutions and some people treat other individuals differently because of an individual's "race." This disparate treatment occurs because the person discriminating believes there are inherent differences between those being discriminated against, and those who are guilty of the discrimination. This belief about inherent differences may or may not precede racial classification, but a system of racial classification sanctions them. A person who did not harbor this belief would assume that such differences are natural, else why would the government use such a classification system?

Because most Americans failed to recognize that racial discrimination and racial classification are two sides of the same coin, many of our laws rely on the same system of racial classifications. For example, the Home Mortgage Disclosure Act (HMDA) requires banks to identify the race of every applicant for a home loan. If the applicant refuses to self-identify their race, the bank is required to make their own judgement about the person's race.

At the same time, the Federal Reserve's Regulation B explicitly prohibits banks from even asking credit card applicants about their race. Given this tangled web, what is a bank to do when a father moves his family into a new area, and applies simultaneously for a home loan and a Visa? And which message does the federal government want to send? Is racial classification appropriate, as HMDA implies, or is it inappropriate, as Regulation B implies?

A Downward Spiral

One of the great thinkers in American history gave a definitive answer. In commenting on the state of black America under Jim Crow, W.E.B. DuBois declared, "When, by proscription and prejudice, . . . Negroes are classed with and treated like the lowest of their people, simply because they are Negroes, such a policy not only discourages thrift and intelligence among black men, but puts a direct premium on the very things you complain of—inefficiency and crime."

A system of racial classification robs those on the wrong side of the classification of the intellectual and moral characteristics necessary for survival. In their drive to gain or maintain race privileges, they focus on things entirely outside their sphere of influence—skin color—and ignore what is within it—individual development. By focusing on things they cannot control or change, they place themselves in a downward spiral. They long for that which they cannot have, and when they don't get it, despair sets in.

Like DuBois, Alexis de Tocqueville's observations on slavery during his sojourn through America have a prophetic ring, as though he were describing our world.

He sees that care for his own fate has not devolved on him; the very use of thought seems to him an unprofitable gift of Providence, and he peacefully enjoys all the privileges of his humiliation. If he becomes free, he often feels independence as a heavier burden than slavery itself, for his life has taught him to submit to everything, except to the dictates of reason; and when reason becomes his only guide, he cannot hear its voice. A thousand new wants assail him, and he lacks the knowledge and the energy needed to resist them. Desires are masters against whom one must fight, and he has learned nothing but to submit and obey. So he has reached this climax of affliction in which slavery brutalizes him and freedom leads him to destruction.

While Tocqueville ascribes this malaise to slavery, a more accurate assessment would target racial classification.

Race in Democracy

In non-democratic societies, maintaining racial classification systems is not very difficult: there are no expectations of equality. But in the Anglo-American tradition, where equality is instinctive, systems of racial classification grate. Although we often have trouble agreeing on what those instincts mean, we really do expect our laws and mores to insure "equal justice before the law."

The central problem of a system of racial classification is that it uses an impermissible criterion to draw lines. Of course, democracy is all about drawing lines; every law draws a line. It may not be possible to express what makes some lines impermissible and other lines merely bad. We might even disagree about whether some lines are impermissible. I am confident, however, that most everyone agrees that lines based on race—that is, systems of racial classification—are impermissible.

Race Is About Power

Whenever race is invoked, it is about power. Whether it was the imposition of the "one-drop" rule on the children of Thomas Jefferson and Sally Hemmings, or India's caste system, race is always about power. To preserve its power, the group establishing the classification system uses a readily identifiable characteristic to separate those with power from those without power. In nearly all cases, skin color, a.k.a. race, is the easiest characteristic to use. By grouping all individuals by race, no one needs to consider people as individuals. Racial classifications turn human beings into mere objects.

Ramirez. © 1995 by Copley News Service. Reproduced by permission.

The classification system reduces people on both sides to the stereotypes created by the system. It simplifies the calculus of individual evaluation by defining away the gray areas. The most venal, lazy sycophant on the right side is, by definition, morally superior to the most caring, hard working person on the wrong side of the system.

23

In America, whites designed and enforced the "one-drop" rule as the governing racial classification system. This "rule" has dominated race relations in America for our entire history. It relegates to the status of blacks anyone with just one drop of black blood. Anyone with "any known African black ancestry" is black. Thus, people like Olympic decathlete Dan O'Brien and Lena Horne, whose skin color is not readily identifiable as "black," are and were black, and subject to the same abuse that someone obviously black may face.

The "one-drop" rule has served various purposes in American history. Slave owners used this rule to insure that the children of their slave mistresses would also be slaves. Public opinion leaders in the South used it to denigrate all black people, and thereby defend slavery.

The authors and enforcers of the Jim Crow system used it to define who could sit at the front of a bus, eat at Woolworth's or vote. Equal employment officers in the public and private sectors use it to determine who is eligible for extra points in awarding of contracts, admissions programs and hiring. Today, the "one-drop" rule is the government's guide for determining who is eligible for various racial preference programs.

Race Is an Illusion

Despite being committed to the "one-drop" rule, and despite the widespread use of racial classification in government programs, Americans generally cannot define what they mean by race. In defining it, they often refer to country of origin, or native tongue. Some people mention religion, others suggest physical characteristics like skin color or hair texture. Regardless of the feature chosen, they are certain that race can be identified scientifically. Indeed, a recent Zogby poll found that 73.2 percent of Americans believe that "race is determined by your genetics," rather than by "societal views and perceptions."

Geneticists and anthropologists are less sanguine about their ability to distinguish races in any systematic fashion. Numerous studies have tried to identify biological characteristics that separate the races. After decades of trying, scientists have concluded that race has no biological component. In fact, scientists have demonstrated that differences within a "race" are greater than the differences between the "races."....

Racial Classification in the 21st Century

As long as government continues to invade Americans' privacy asking them to identify their race, we will continue to segregate Americans, and sap the strength of people on both sides of the line. We cannot erase America's racial lines until people know that skin color cannot play a role in public life. And as long as government keeps asking people about their race, Americans will always suspect that race plays a role.

Eliminating the race boxes from American public life has many advantages. It gets government out of the business of defining races, a task, as we have seen, for which government is wholly unsuited. Even the latest policy of having individuals self-identify their race does not solve this problem. People still need some guidance to understand what the various choices offered to them mean. If each person checking a race box understood the choices differently, the data gathered would be meaningless.

Eliminating these boxes from our government forms also allows Americans to protect their racial privacy. Perhaps most importantly, eliminating the race boxes allows America to clear the final hurdle in our journey to fulfill the democratic dreams of our greatest statesmen.

This is the next step in America's quest to eradicate race from our national psyche. Until the race boxes are gone, we will continue to damn generations of black people. As has always been true, a few people will succeed despite the chains, but the vast majority can never fulfill their full potential until we renounce racial classification.

"Race information is more helpful than not."

Racial Classifications Should Not Be Abandoned

Emil Guillermo

In the following viewpoint Emil Guillermo contends that maintaining data regarding race helps minorities. Without racial data, he argues, it would be impossible to document racial profiling or to provide appropriate health screening in cases of race-specific diseases. Keeping track of racial statistics, Guillermo asserts, prevents racism from continuing unchecked. Emil Guillermo, a radio and TV commentator, is author of *Amok: Essays from an Asian-American Perspective.*

As you read, consider the following questions:
1. Why does Guillermo call himself a "demographer's nightmare"?
2. Why did the police officer ask Guillermo his race when he pulled him over for speeding?
3. According to the author, where does Ward Connerly claim that racial data would be obtained if the Racial Privacy Initiative passed?

M ay is time for ethnic celebration. Cinco De Mayo is just
one day. But the whole month is Asian Pacific American Heritage Month. Get out the egg rolls, and let's party!

In government offices at the state and local levels, events that mix culture and history will take place throughout the month. . . .

But if the prevailing attitude of the Racial Privacy Initiative [RPI] takes over, they won't be happening for long.

Race Censorship

The RPI means RIP [rest in peace] for such festivities, and, by law, government workers will be left with a May known as (CENSORED)-American Heritage Month, a month dedicated to all the (CENSORED)-American people in our community.

Sound like good, clean American fun?

Just don't call it race censorship.

It's the world of race privacy, the latest scam from the mind of Ward Connerly. He's black, but apparently that's his business and no one else's. The man who gave us Prop. 209, the so-called Civil Rights Initiative, which in reality outlawed government-based affirmative action in the state in 1996, has returned with the next phase in his color-blinding of California.

Connerly's collected nearly a million signatures in support of the initiative, and it could be on the [California] ballot as early as November [2002]. At this stage, a Field Poll taken last week showed that nearly 48 percent of California's voters back the measure.[1]

The idea is simple and extremely deceptive in its appeal.

If it were passed, the Race Privacy Initiative would ban any classification by race. Proud about being Hispanic? Black? Asian? Keep it to yourself. No one would care anymore. And no one would ask you. No more questions on state forms. No more of those "check the box" items. The new initiative would, if signed into law, force you to put a bag over your head (hopefully, not a brown one, but a nice

1. The Racial Privacy Initiative was rejected by the voters of California on October 7, 2003.

neutral color)—and make it against the law for anyone to peek.

The basic pitch is privacy, and, in these days, when there seems to be so little of it, it's a winning ploy.

Race Makes a Difference in Treatment

• The Food and Drug Administration is expected to approve the drug BiDil in June [2005], making it the first "ethnic drug" on the market. After failing in a broader study, BiDil was shown to be effective in treating heart failure in a clinical study that included only African-Americans.

• African-Americans need higher doses of one medication used to treat asthma than Caucasians, suggesting "an inherent predisposition" in blacks not to absorb the medicine as easily, says a study in the February [2005] issue of the journal *Chest*.

Gregory M. Lamb, *Christian Science Monitor*, March 3, 2005.

"Tired of being asked?" Connerly's American Civil Rights Coalition muses on its Web site. "It seems like every time we fill out a government form, the snooping bureaucracy wants to know: 'What are you? What's your race?' Why should it matter to the government?"

Even I am lured by that pitch.

More Helpful than Not

I hate checking the box on government forms, but less out of concern for my privacy and more because of my desire for accuracy. As a Filipino American with a Spanish surname, I'm a demographer's nightmare. Asian? Hispanic? On the census, I mark "other" and write-in "Aspanic."

But race information is more helpful than not. A short time ago, your humble columnist was stopped by a police officer for speeding. Principles of the free market do not extend to driving. After the standard ticketing process, the officer asked me about my race. I was totally taken aback by the question—angry, even (though perhaps I was more angered by the speeding ticket). Later, after successfully contesting the ticket in court (the officer hadn't used a cali-

28

brated radar gun), I learned that having law enforcement ask the racial question is the only way for the government to find out whether, over a period of time, the law stopped ethnic drivers more than whites. If we drive while color-blind, how will we know whether the CHP [California Highway Patrol] is protecting our rights or violating them?

Race privacy would not only affect affirmative action—it would also seriously hamper efforts to research the profiling issue, of any policy issue. Little wonder, then, that researchers and policy analysts have been among those most critical of the initiative so far. Doing government-funded research on heart disease in the community? You wouldn't be able to ask your subjects about race or ethnic background. Research on poverty? Employment? Housing? You name it. Any possible inquiry impacted by race or ethnicity would be stymied.

Of course, without knowing race and ethnicity, how could we have identified such simple public-health issues as the Asian-American community's tendency toward high blood pressure?

Race privacy would make it impossible to uncover the changing needs of the state. Send in English-speaking doctors to administer to the newly arrived Hmong? Do we need native speakers or translators in certain areas? How will we know?

To paraphrase that old Clintonian phrase, "It's the data, stupid."

Privacy or Invisibility?

Connerly says you can get what you need from the census. But you certainly wouldn't find the specific data of particular individuals involved in unique studies. In his desire to kill affirmative action, a highly targeted approach to remedying disparities in education and employment, Connerly gets rid of race as a factor in just about everything else.

The Racial Privacy Initiative says to the growing ethnic majority population of California, "The less we know about you, the better. Just as you become the dominant force in the state, go hide under a rock. And stay there."

In the old days, society could merely ignore ethnic populations. Now, under the cover of "privacy," Connerly makes

knowing nothing about ethnic communities seem less discriminatory than it really is.

Ah, color blindness. What a wonderful world it would be,
filled with ignorance and invisibility, two essential ingredi-
ents for racism. That's the ultimate outcome of Connerly's
deceptive vision.

"Why must we deny or hide parts of our racial makeup because of historical reasons or because it makes others feel bad?"

The Multiracial Classification Is Necessary

Eve Brown

In the following viewpoint Eve Brown maintains that a single racial designation cannot accurately define the identity of a mixed-race person. Identifying herself as multiracial does not mean that she is denigrating or denying her black heritage, Brown claims. Rather, she asserts, it means striving for an honest and inclusive self-definition. Ultimately, argues Brown, the decision to label oneself as multiracial is not a political decision but an individual choice. Eve Brown writes for *Raising Black and Biracial Children*.

As you read, consider the following questions:

1. Why does Brown conclude that the saleswoman does not like to be called "Red"?
2. Why, according to the author, do some blacks frown upon the multiracial designation?
3. As a multiracial person, how does the author answer the question "What's wrong with just being black"?

Eve Brown, "Mixed Blessings: What's Wrong with Just Being Black?" *Raising Black and Biracial Children*, April 30, 2002, p. 32. Reproduced by permission.

There's nothing wrong with just being black. My son is black, although he also has a percentage of my French and Native American ancestry, as well as his father's (my ex-husband's) African American ancestry. But I was asked this by a black woman who was selling me a pair of shoes for my son. She took me by surprise because she initially asked me about my racial heritage. When I told her I was black, French, and Native American, she quickly said I must be Creole. And then she went on about how a female co-worker was Creole too and how people didn't know how to act with her because they didn't know what race she was (sad, but true). She kept talking about this while I just listened for the most part. It turned out to be one of those interchanges that just begs for deeper reflection.

I have to wonder though if she would have so quickly identified me as "Creole" or inquired about my heritage if I didn't have my infant son there too. He looks "white," as his father (my husband) is white. But from the moment she started serving us until I had paid for the shoes and was preparing to leave, it was she who pursued this subject with me.

In fact, I was a little wary at first because I wasn't sure if this was going to be one of those friendly inquiries or a disapproving monologue. And I'm always concerned about what my older son gleans from such instances. I could tell that she had some questions; I just never thought it would be, "What's wrong with just being black?"

Most people are curious about what it's like to be multiracial or, at the very least, as this saleswoman had begun, about our racial makeup. But she had a point she wanted to make and she already knew what it's like to be "Creole" from her "Creole" co-worker. I'm just sorry that I didn't have the time to spend with her so that I could have explained a few things to her. This is something I've thought long and hard about, even before she asked it.

I can't find fault with her question or the underlying feelings she was expressing. There was something very genuine about this question and her tone of voice as she asked it. Some people call her "Red," she explained, because of her skin tone. She did have a reddish tinge to her beautiful brown tone, but she didn't like being called "Red." And that's when she asked, "What's wrong with just being black?"

Her question implied many things. Foremost, she was proud to be just black. That's great! I'm glad for her—to be proud to be just black but our racial identity is only one aspect of ourselves. She couldn't understand why some multiracial people, being part black, just don't say they are black. So, I kind of think she didn't like my answer.

Torn Between Two Races

Being biracial can sometimes leave you feeling somewhat torn. . . . I used to get frustrated because I felt that I was not Chinese enough or Jewish enough. . . . What box am I supposed to check for race? I can only check one—and if I do, I will deny the other. . . . Well there is always the infamous "other" box. . . .

Although we live in a world where everyone won't accept you, you need to learn to accept yourself.

Two races, one face.

What am I? Proud.

Emerald Katz, *Asian Week*, May 10–16, 2002.

But another message this saleswoman was conveying was that she feels belittled as a black person when some blacks of mixed parentage want to include their other ancestries into their racial identity. Historically, blacks in this country have been treated like they were the least desirable people on earth, supposedly because of their race. We have since learned that it was to justify our system of slavery. But the agony, of course, is the ongoing damage and bigotry.

So, I do understand and respect this saleswoman's perspective and feelings. After all, being part black, I too have experienced such racism and know the agony. Multiracial people cannot escape that, not really. But that is the real issue here, whether we are trying to escape racism by including our other ancestries in our racial identity.

Many blacks feel we are trying to distance ourselves from the racial and social history we share with them. And they then fear that we are going to end up collaborating with the "oppressors" against them. They, of course, especially feel this way if one of our other races is white. So, by asking "what's wrong with just being black?" is really asking "why are you ashamed of being black?"

First of all, black people have done absolutely nothing wrong to have caused them to be subjected to slavery and racism in this country. They were innocent victims. Secondly, because we identify ourselves as multiracial doesn't mean we are necessarily ashamed of being black.

And finally, identifying ourselves as biracial or multiracial people doesn't mean we are distancing ourselves from other black people or denying our black heritage. Rather, many of us want to bring "our people" with us on our journey to the racially harmonious society we envision.

An Individual Choice

So getting back to the basic question of "What's wrong with just being black?" Nothing—unless you are also another race and wish to identify yourself inclusively. This saleswoman must have been anticipating this response from me because after asking that question, she promptly added that most black people, especially in this country, are multiracial and ". . . even some white people are multiracial." I corrected her on that point, and said that yes, many whites are multinational as well as multiethnic, but not multiracial. She then said that if they checked into it, many whites would discover, in fact, that other races are represented in their genealogy. I had to agree with her there, and even used my infant son as an example, for many "white" people blend into the white race undetected, so to speak. But that was beside the point.

The point is this—regardless of all the above concerns— we multiracial people have the right to make an individual choice about our racial identity. Just because it, at the same time, may threaten many blacks because of ongoing historical issues doesn't mean we should deny our white or other ancestries. We should not necessarily flaunt it, but we certainly should not deny it.

Need we be making a political statement when we identity ourselves as multiracial? For many of us, it is merely a personal choice devoid of political intent. However, if we choose to become politically active regarding this issue, that's our choice too and should be respected by others. Voting and politicking are voluntary activities. Not all of us want to be bothered with the politics of race.

Who We Are

Some may argue that we can't avoid the political repercussions of our choice to identify ourselves as "multiracial" on various forms, thereby placing us against blacks who are trying to gain political concessions for their "members." But wait a minute! First of all, who says we won't be counted as among blacks. Secondly, what the government or anyone else does with our racial categorization is a separate issue. Obviously, it is one that needs to be addressed and some of us are attempting to resolve this issue through our politicking. But others of us don't really care but still identify ourselves as "multiracial." And lastly, why should we be concerned with their need for our "numbers" when they don't recognize that we have the need to be who we are?

It's not a matter of needing to be different either. IT'S WHO WE ARE. Most of us aren't trying to be different; we're just being who we are and we just happen to be different.

What's wrong with just being multiracial? Why must we deny or hide parts of our racial makeup because of historical reasons or because it makes others feel bad? What is important is our own comfort with our identity as we choose to define it. We are the ones who will be most affected by it. After all, shouldn't our ultimate priority be our individual selves—our personal and psychological well-being? Not the political well-being of the black race?

The Well-Being of All

As it is, I'm not only concerned with the well-being of the black race. It is my opinion that people only concerned with themselves are never truly happy people. I'm concerned with the well-being of the entire human race. But it takes mutual respect and understanding for there to be racial harmony, provided racial harmony is everyone's goal. I entered into that conversation with that saleswoman, albeit warily, because I was thinking, "Oh here is an enlightened black woman." But from the beginning she stereotyped me in her own mind as your typical, uppity "Creole" who thought she was better than other blacks. I'm not better, just different. Although I was willing to give her the benefit of the doubt, she wasn't willing to give the same to me. Yes, I understand and respect her perspective and feelings, but sadly she couldn't do the same for me.

"It would be regrettable if the progressive aims of the mixed race movement led to the elimination of all racial data."

The Multiracial Classification Can Be Detrimental

Frank H. Wu

In the following viewpoint Frank H. Wu asserts that allowing the multiracial classification on government forms can in fact harm the very people it strives to help. If people who would formerly have identified themselves as members of a minority group instead call themselves multiracial, Wu argues, gathering statistics to prove racial discrimination will become difficult. Wu is a law professor at Howard University in Washington, D.C.

As you read, consider the following questions:
1. According to sociologists that Wu cites, what percentage of African Americans are of mixed heritage?
2. How did the NAACP justify their campaign to "check the black box"?
3. Why would it be regrettable, in Wu's opinion, if the mixed race movement led to the elimination of all racial data?

Mixed race individuals have existed since before the nation was founded, but the mixed race movement is new. In 1896, Homer Plessy challenged state-sanctioned racial segregation before the Supreme Court. When he lost his case, the decision established the legality of the Jim Crow system. What started as open white supremacy remade itself through the falsehood of the phrase "separate but equal" until that fiction could no longer be sustained. The ruling against Plessy is all the more remarkable because Plessy himself was an "octoroon," who had seven great-grandparents who were white and only one great-grandparent who was black. But Plessy would have to ride in the "colored" compartment of the train, and, eventually, his descendants would be relegated to the back of the bus and the decrepit schoolhouse.

Attitudes Toward Mixed Race Children

Mixed race individuals were formerly shunned. They were especially despised if their mothers were white. Under the rule of white supremacy mixed race children took the subordinate race as theirs. Thus, a white woman could give birth to a black baby, but a black woman could not give birth to a white baby. The arrival of neither mixed race child would be celebrated. (As African American novelist James Baldwin once said to a white segregationist about these unstated rules, "You're not worried about me marrying *your* daughter." He explained, "You're worried about me marrying your *wife's* daughter. I've been marrying your daughter ever since the days of slavery.")

Because they engender confusion about categories, mixed race individuals destabilize a universal order in which all know their place and stay there. White attitudes toward mixed race individuals have oscillated between extremes, with animal husbandry providing the analogy in both cases. Expert dog breeder Leon Fradley, who wrote *The Complete Book of Dog Care*, was also a eugenicist who wrote *The Case for Sterilization* and praised Adolf Hitler for carrying out sterilization on a wide scale. Philanthropist Elroy Stock had his gift to Augsburg College returned in 1988 after he was discovered to be the author of thousands of unsigned letters sent to strangers in a campaign targeting people in mixed marriages and who had adopted children of other races; one of his primary arguments to the strangers whom he terrified was, "A dog breeder would not think of producing mongrel dogs, so why should the human race be mongrel?" The depictions of mixed race individuals have been contradictory, but all contained a monstrous aspect. They were commonly looked upon as the incarnation of crossbred degeneracy, the exemplars of dangerous tendencies toward racial amalgamation. Less often they were viewed as the embodiment of hybrid vigor, experiments in propagating the best of two types. In any event, they were frightening because they could lead to the extinction of the white race, but they also were rumored to be sterile like mules. . . .

Mixed Race America

Sociologists who have studied the matter are confident that one-quarter to one-third of African Americans are of mixed heritage, not to mention many whites who have never doubted their own absolute whiteness. Frederick Douglass, Booker T. Washington, W.E.B. DuBois, Philip Randolph, Martin Luther King Jr., Malcolm X, Kwame Anthony Appiah, and Lani Guinier all had white parents or grandparents. Alex Haley's family history, *Roots*, was a best-selling book and one of the first television mini-series. Novelist Ishmael Reed has said of Haley's account of his slave ancestry, "If [he] had traced his father's bloodline, he would have traveled twelve generations back to, not Gambia, but *Ireland*." Gregory Howard Williams, dean of the Ohio State University law school, believed he was white and his father was Italian, until he was ten years old. His book, *Life on the Color Line: The True Story of How a White Boy Discovered He Was Black* (1995), is one of three recent autobiographies penned by law professors about their mixed race status, part of a new genealogical specialty in race relations literature that attests to our sudden willingness to discuss, to borrow the title of journalist Edward Ball's National Book Award–winning work, "slaves in the family."

A century after *Plessy* and in imitation of the 1963 March on Washington of the civil rights movement, the mixed race movement gathered in 1996 at the nation's capital to demand equality. Organized by *Interracial Voice* magazine, the rally attracted only a few hundred people despite the burgeoning numbers of mixed race individuals. According to the 2000 Census, there are about 1,655,830 mixed race individuals who are part Asian. They make up almost one in seven of the total number of Asian Americans and about one in a quarter of all mixed race persons.

Racial Categories and the Census

I would strongly recommend a tabulation process [for the U.S. Census] that would look at the various combinations and then place them in enforcement categories. For example, if you have someone who is half African-American and half white, and if you look at the historic discrimination problems that people have had in our society—whether it's in employment, admissions into colleges and universities, securing government contracts or living in communities where they've had redlining or whatever—the conclusion you would draw is that somebody who is half white and half black would be discriminated against if they applied for a bank loan, because of (being) half black. You want to make sure that, as we look at the historic need for enforcement against discrimination, you recognize that that person is part African-American.

Daryl Lindsey, *Salon*, February 2, 2000.

The mixed race movement, with advocacy groups such as Reclassify All Children Equally (RACE), has had a much stronger political effect than the numbers of those directly involved might suggest. Its rhetoric is based more on personal liberty and human dignity than on scientific precision or historical accuracy. Central to its crusade are photographic portraits of mixed race people and personal stories about busybodies asking "How did you come by that name?" demanding to know, "Which are you more of?" or being told by white cousins, "You're so normal," or, for light-skinned individuals "You're no more black than I am." The principal claim of the mixed race movement is that individuals should be allowed to define themselves, either by designating themselves as belonging to as many official classifications as each person wishes or by refusing to participate in the classificatory scheme altogether. It has appropriated the term "hapa haole," a Hawaiian word for "half white," which has had derogatory connotations and made "hapa" more dignified.

The Mixed Race Movement

The mixed race movement won a partial victory with the 2000 Census. . . . Mixed race persons were not asked to accept their place in an arbitrary taxonomy by bureaucratic mandate or for a rigid consistency with a black and white worldview. The Office of Management and Budget worked out a compromise. As another indication of the illusory quality of race, the Census has modified racial classifications regularly, never using the same system for any two consecutive decades. This time, although the Census form did not include a new multiracial category, people could check off as many boxes as they wished and they would not be assigned to a race by surveyors. The several boxes produced sixty-three permutations.

Defying expectations, as it grew the mixed race movement found few allies among established community organizations such as the National Association for the Advancement of Colored People (NAACP). The Congressional Black Caucus conducted a forty-two-city tour urging African Americans to "check the black box." They enlisted Black Entertainment Television host Tavis Smiley, radio personality Tom Joyner, and black preachers to remind African Americans that they were once counted as only three-fifths of a person and suggested that only by checking a single box would they be accorded their full status as a person. The director of the effort, Kristen Haggins, explained, "Checking more than one box on the Census could prove to dilute our count and also dilute our potential for receiving money for our communities and impact how boundaries are drawn politically."

Although the plea of mixed race individuals for self-determination is easy to accept, the NAACP also can hardly be faulted for having subverted the white tenet that any black ancestry turns a person black. The NAACP is turning this tenet into an organizing principle for the benefit not of whites but of blacks. The very people of mixed race backgrounds whom whites refused to accept as their own could be enlisted among blacks, each addition being another voter in democratic elections. But the tactic has an uncertain future, because it depends on people of mixed race backgrounds continuing to lack autonomy.

The unintended consequences of the mixed race movement are already apparent. There are broader and deeper issues at stake. Former House Speaker Newt Gingrich supported the multiracial category, but only because he wanted to purge all racial counting. Conservative leader Ward Connerly has mounted a California initiative campaign in an attempt to accomplish that very goal. Even Connerly has admitted that people laugh at him if he claims to be Irish based on his three-eighths Irish blood, which constitutes the largest proportion of his background. Whatever his ideology, Connerly is perceived of as black.

Eradicating Labels, Obscuring Problems

It would be regrettable if the progressive aims of the mixed race movement led to the elimination of all racial data. Ironically, efforts to determine the effects of racial discrimination must label individuals by race. Racial data can ameliorate the feelings of coercion by allowing self-definition. The opposition to compiling racial data of any type is misguided at best and misleading at worst. Connerly implies that the racial problem is the data rather than the reality and that eradicating information will eradicate problems. Others offer an inflammatory but inappropriate comparison of Census requirements with the Nazi Nuremberg laws or the South African apartheid regime, drawing a parallel that is plausible only if racism and its remedies are rendered equivalent.

Paradoxically, color blindness requires color consciousness. Racial numbers substantiate racial disparities. Without numbers, it becomes impossible to measure if a society has progressed toward integration or to corroborate the existence of racial discrimination. For example, it would become difficult to present objective evidence that African Americans are underrepresented among state government employees compared to their proportions within the general population or compared to the qualified pool of job applicants, or that African Americans and other people of color are the victims of disparities in the criminal justice system that can be explained by nothing other than racial factors. Statistics cannot prevent people from making decisions based on race, but they make it possible to prove that people have done so. Without data, however imperfect, issues of race cannot even be analyzed intelligently. Nobody would suggest a similar strategy in any other context. If the National Weather Service stopped tracking tornadoes, they would not stop touching down.

If nothing else, the mixed race movement has won over companies that would like to please a wide range of potential consumers. In 1996, the General Mills conglomerate unveiled a new face for its Betty Crocker brand name. Using a computer, designers gave the iconic homemaker a painstaking makeover by using the profiles of 75 women of various races to generate a composite.

> "*The traditional values of American identity . . . are deeply at odds with radical, de-civilizing tenets of the 'multiculturalist' enterprise.*"

Multiculturalism Threatens American Culture

Roger Kimball

Multiculturalism, Roger Kimball argues in the following viewpoint, is destroying American unity. According to Kimball, multiculturalism devalues Western ideals in order to appease minority groups. As a result, Kimball argues, minorities are encouraged to identify with their ethnic groups rather than band together as Americans. Kimball asserts that all Americans should return to the ideal of unity that America's founding fathers embraced. Kimball is managing editor of the *New Criterion*.

As you read, consider the following questions:

1. According to Kimball, what is the effect of multiculturalism on education?
2. What words did Kimball find lacking in Maya Angelou's 1992 inaugural poem?
3. What case does the author make against the "lowly hyphen"?

Roger Kimball, "Institutionalizing Our Demise: America vs. Multiculturalism," *The New Criterion*, vol. 22, June 2004. Copyright © 2004 by *The New Criterion*. Reproduced by permission.

The widespread sense of condign outrage—of horror leavened by anger and elevated by resolve—testified to a renewed sense of national purpose and identity after [the terrorist attacks of September 11, 2001]. Attacked, many Americans suddenly (if temporarily) rediscovered the virtue of patriotism. At the beginning of his remarkable book *Who Are We? The Challenges to America's National Identity* (2004), the Harvard political scientist Samuel Huntington recalls a certain block on Charles Street in Boston. At one time, American flags flew in front of a U.S. Post Office and a liquor store. Then the Post Office stopped displaying the flag, so on September 11, 2001, the flag was flying only in front of the liquor store. Within two weeks, seventeen American flags decorated that block of Charles Street, in addition to a huge flag suspended over the street close by. "With their country under attack," Huntington notes, "Charles Street denizens rediscovered their nation and identified themselves with it."

Was that rediscovery anything more than a momentary passion? Huntington reports that within a few months, the flags on Charles Street began to disappear. By the time the first anniversary rolled around in September 2002, only four were left flying. True, that is four times more than were there on September 10, 2001, but it is less than a quarter of the number that populated Charles Street at the end of September 2001.

Cultural Dissolution

There are similar anecdotes from around the country—an access of flag-waving followed by a relapse into indifference. Does it mean that the sudden upsurge of patriotism in the weeks following 9/11 was only, as it were, skin deep? Or perhaps it merely testifies to the fact that a sense of permanent emergency is difficult to maintain, especially in the absence of fresh attacks. Is our sense of ourselves as Americans patent only when challenged? "Does it," Huntington asks, "take an Osama bin Laden . . . to make us realize that we are Americans? If we do not experience recurring destructive attacks, will we return to the fragmentation and eroded Americanism before September 11?"

One hopes that the answer is No. . . . But I fear that for every schoolchild standing at attention for the National Anthem, there is a teacher or lawyer or judge or politician or ACLU [American Civil Liberties Union] employee militating against the hegemony of the dominant culture, the insupportable intrusion of white, Christian, "Eurocentric" values into the curriculum, the school pageant, the town green, etc., etc. The demonstration of national character and resolve following September 11 was extraordinary. It did not, however, purchase immunity from the virus of cultural dissolution. . . .

Those forces are not isolated phenomena; they are not even confined to America. They are part of a global crisis in national identity, coefficients of the sudden collapse of self-confidence in the West—a collapse that shows itself in everything from swiftly falling birthrates in "old Europe" to the attack on the whole idea of the sovereign nation state. It is hard to avoid thinking that a people that has lost the will to reproduce or govern itself is a people on the road to destruction.

An Anti-Western Ideology

Only a few years ago we were invited to contemplate the pleasant spectacle of the "end of history" and the establishment of Western-style liberal democracy, attended by the handmaidens of prosperity and rising standards of health care and education, the world over. Things look rather different now as a variety of centrifugal forces threatens to undermine the sources of national identity and, with it, the sources of national strength and the security which that strength underwrites.

The threat shows itself in many ways, from culpable complacency to the corrosive imperatives of "multiculturalism" and political correctness. (I use scare quotes because what generally travels under the name of "multiculturalism" is really a form of monocultural animus directed against the dominant culture.) In essence, as Huntington notes, multiculturalism is "anti-European civilization. . . . It is basically an anti-Western ideology." The multiculturalists claim to be fostering a progressive cultural cosmopolitanism distinguished by superior sensitivity to the downtrodden and dispossessed. In fact, they encourage an orgy of self-flagellating liberal guilt as impotent as it is insatiable. The "sensitivity" of the multiculturalist is an index not of moral refinement but of moral vacuousness. As the French essayist Pascal Bruckner observed, "An overblown conscience is an empty conscience."

Compassion ceases if there is nothing but compassion, and revulsion turns to insensitivity. Our "soft pity," as Stefan Zweig calls it, is stimulated, because guilt is a convenient substitute for action where action is impossible. Without the power to do anything, sensitivity becomes our main aim. The aim is not so much to do anything, as to be judged. Salvation lies in the verdict that declares us to be wrong. Multiculturalism is a moral intoxicant; its thrill centers around the emotion of superior virtue; its hangover subsists on a diet of nescience and blighted "good intentions.". . .

A profound ignorance of the milestones of American culture is one predictable result of this mood. The statistics have become proverbial. Huntington quotes one poll from the 1990s showing that while 90 percent of Ivy League students could identify Rosa Parks, only 25 percent could identify the author of the words "government of the people, by the people, for the people." (Yes, it's the Gettysburg Address.) In a 1999 survey, 40 percent of seniors at fifty-five top colleges could not say within half a century when the Civil War was fought. Another study found that more high school students knew who Harriet Tubman was than knew that Washington commanded the American army in the revolution or that Abraham Lincoln wrote the Emancipation Proclamation. Doubtless you have your own favorite horror story.

Not Only an Academic Phenomenon

But multiculturalism is not only an academic phenomenon. The attitudes it fosters have profound social as well as intellectual consequences. One consequence has been a sharp rise in the phenomenon of immigration without—or with only partial—assimilation: a dangerous demographic trend that threatens American identity in the most basic way.

These various agents of dissolution are also elements in a wider culture war: the contest to define how we live and what counts as the good in the good life. Anti-Americanism occupies such a prominent place on the agenda of the culture wars precisely because the traditional values of American identity—articulated by the Founders and grounded in a commitment to individual liberty and public virtue—are deeply at odds with the radical, de-civilizing tenets of the "multiculturalist" enterprise.

Americans Are Failing American History

• Four out of five—81%—of seniors from the top 55 colleges and universities in the United States . . . could not identify Valley Forge, or words from the Gettysburg Address, or even the basic principles of the U.S. Constitution.

• Scarcely more than half knew general information about American democracy and the Constitution.

• Only 34% of the students surveyed could identify George Washington as an American general at the battle of Yorktown, the culminating battle of the American Revolution.

• Only 42% were able to identify George Washington as "First in war, first in peace, first in the hearts of his countrymen."

• Less than one quarter (23%) correctly identified James Madison as the "father of the Constitution."

American Council of Trustees and Alumni, "Losing America's Memory: Historical Illiteracy in the 21st Century," ACTA Web site, February 16, 2000. www.goacta.org.

To get a sense of what has happened to the institution of American identity, compare Robert Frost's performance at John F. Kennedy's inauguration in 1961 with Maya Angelou's performance thirty-two years later. As Huntington reminds us, Frost spoke of the "heroic deeds" of America's founding, an event, he said, that with "God's approval" ushered in "a new order of the ages." By contrast, Maya Angelou never mentioned the words "America" or "American." Instead, she identified twenty-seven ethnic or religious groups that had suffered repression because of America's "armed struggles for profit," "cynicism," and "brutishness."

Repellent though Maya Angelou's performance was, it did seem the appropriate rhetorical embroidery to welcome Bill Clinton, a president infatuated with the blandishments of multiculturalism and who sought a third "great revolution" to emancipate America from the legacy of European civilization and its Anglo-Protestant values. It has to be acknowledged that considerable progress toward that goal was made during his administration.

The Lowly Hyphen

A favorite weapon in the armory of multiculturalism is the lowly hyphen. When we speak of an African-American or Mexican-American or Asian-American these days, the aim is not descriptive but deconstructive. There is a polemical edge to it, a provocation. The hyphen does not mean "American, but hailing at some point in the past from someplace else." It means "only provisionally American: my allegiance is divided at best." (I believe something similar can be said about the feminist fad for hyphenating the bride's maiden name with her husband's surname. It is a gesture of independence that is also a declaration of divided loyalty.) It is curious to what extent the passion for hyphenation is fostered more by the liberal elite than the populations it is supposedly meant to serve. How does it serve them? Presumably by enhancing their sense of "self-esteem." Frederick Douglass saw through this charade some one hundred and fifty years ago. "No one idea," he wrote, "has given rise to more oppression and persecution toward colored people of this country than that which makes Africa, not America, their home."

The indispensable Ward Connerly would agree. Connerly has campaigned vigorously against affirmative action in California. This of course has made him a pariah among the politically correct elite. It has also resulted in some humorous exchanges, such as this telephone interview with a reporter from *The New York Times* in 1997.

Reporter: What are you?

Connerly: I am an American.

Reporter: No, no, no! What *are* you?

Connerly: Yes, yes, yes. I am an American.

Reporter: That is not what I mean. I was told that you are African American. Are you ashamed to be African American?

Connerly: No, I am just proud to be an American.

Connerly went on to explain that his ancestry included Africans, French, Irish, and American Indians. It was too much for the poor reporter from our Paper of Record: "What does that make you?" he asked in uncomprehending exasperation. I suspect he was not edified by Connerly's cheerful response: "That makes me all-American."

The multicultural passion for hyphenation is not simply a fondness for syntactical novelty. It also bespeaks a commitment to the centrifugal force of anti-American tribalism. . . .

A Glorious Opportunity

As the twenty-first century begins, we have a glorious opportunity—perhaps it is the last such opportunity—to start replenishing some of the moral capital we have been so profligate with in recent decades. Some sages assure us that our fate is sealed, that inevitable forces have scripted the (unhappy) denouement of American civilization. I do not believe them. . . .

Samuel Huntington urges us to foster "those qualities that have defined America since its founding," above all the Anglo-Protestant values that wed liberty to order. Many in the liberal, multicultural establishment have rejected Huntington's vision of American unity as nativist or worse. I believe that his critics are wrong. Benjamin Franklin got to the nub of the matter when, more than two hundred years ago, he observed that "We must all hang together or assuredly we shall all hang separately."

> *"Multiculturalism . . . is part of a broader movement to create a more equitable society."*

Multicultural Education Is Vital to the Fabric of America

Gregory Michie

In the wake of the terrorist attacks of September 11, 2001, multiculturalism is more relevant and important than ever, claims Gregory Michie in the following viewpoint. The heart of the multicultural debate, he maintains, centers around education. Teaching courses that promote empathy and awareness of racial and cultural differences, Michie argues, is essential. Multiculturalism, he asserts, means fighting racism and injustice in order to build a more equitable society. Gregory Michie is assistant professor in the Department of Curriculum and Instruction at Illinois State University.

As you read, consider the following questions:

1. During what decade does Michie contend that multiculturalism gained widespread acceptance?
2. What subject did opponents of multiculturalism want to stress in schools after September 11, in the author's opinion?
3. What does Michie feel is his advantage when it comes to teaching students about racism?

Gregory Michie, "All Together Now," *Teacher Magazine*, February 2002. Reproduced by permission of Editorial Projects in Education and the author.

W hen I agreed to teach a Diversity course in a program for future teachers in the summer of 1998, I wasn't sure what I'd gotten myself into. I first witnessed racial intolerance at a young age—growing up in North Carolina during the early years of school desegregation—so I'd long believed that educating about human differences should be an integral part of what schools do. And I'd taught 7th and 8th graders in Chicago since 1990, so I'd also seen first-hand how issues of race, class, culture, and language impact children's lives, both inside and outside the classroom. But how to pass these understandings on to prospective teachers was something I hadn't much considered.

Passing on Understanding

Before I took over, the class was known as Multiculturalism, and the course catalog stated that it was designed to focus on "celebrating the varied ethnic composition" of students in urban schools. Despite this sunny description, racial tensions had boiled over in the class during the summer of '97, resulting in hard feelings and deep divisions among some participants. The situation was so tense that the program's director considered dropping the course from the next summer's schedule. When I offered to give it a shot, he relented.

Some may wonder, why offer a class on multiculturalism at all? If young people want to be teachers, why not give them a head start on lesson planning or instructional methods or classroom management—something they can use?

Certainly such practical matters are important, but teaching is about much more than mastering a set of technical skills. With classrooms across the United States becoming ever more diverse racially, culturally, and linguistically, young teachers also need to deepen their "multicultural competence"—their understanding of their own cultural frames of reference and their ability to reach students from a variety of backgrounds. But just what this multicultural component of teacher preparation should look like has been the subject of much debate.

Born in the 1970s out of the civil rights struggle, the multicultural movement spent much of the '80s being dogged by critics on both the right and the left. But the political correctness of the '90s brought widespread acceptance and, with it, a predictable watering down of multiculturalism's more radical elements. By decade's end, the term had been adopted by so many textbook publishers, school districts, and professional-development consultants that it didn't mean much of anything. As with phrases like "children first," it became ubiquitous, non-threatening, and—ultimately—empty.

The terrorist attacks of September 11, 2001, changed all that, thrusting multiculturalism back into the political crossfire. The terrorist attacks reinvigorated those on both sides of the divide, arousing supporters and detractors alike to re-stake their ground and refresh their arguments. "Those people who said we don't need multiculturalism, that it's too touchy-feely, a pox on them," Judith Rizzo, deputy chancellor for instruction in New York City's public schools, told a conference audience while discussing bias incidents shortly after the attacks. "I think they've learned their lesson. We have to do more to teach habits of tolerance, knowledge, and awareness of other cultures."

But if opponents of multicultural education indeed had learned their lesson, they weren't letting on. If anything, they were circling the wagons. Lynne Cheney, wife of Vice President Dick Cheney, said in a speech to the Dallas Institute of Humanities and Culture that, rather than embracing multiculturalism, schools should place a stronger emphasis on teaching American history. And Diane Ravitch, in an *Education Week* commentary in October 2001, blasted the notion that a renewed commitment to multicultural education was an appropriate response to the tragedy. "The implication is that this unprecedented atrocity was caused by a failure in the schools' curriculum, rather than by heartless, inhumane terrorists," Ravitch wrote. She added later: "I suggest that what our schools must do is teach young people the virtues and blessings of our democratic system of government. Our ability to defend what we hold dear depends on our knowledge and understanding of it."

Lots of Flags

In the weeks following the attacks on the World Trade Center and the Pentagon, I visited several elementary schools to observe new teachers, and I didn't see much evidence that Ravitch and Cheney need worry. What I saw instead were lots of flags. Big flags, little flags, quilted flags, painted flags. The flag frenzy was so intense that a friend who teaches in a predominantly Mexican American community—and who doesn't display the Stars and Stripes in her classroom—got a letter of reprimand from a substitute who'd taken exception to her apparent lack of patriotic spirit. "Your students look to you for direction," the note concluded. "In the mist [sic] of a national crisis our schools must instill unity in our students." It was the first time I'd ever heard of a teacher being admonished by a sub, but I guess I shouldn't have been surprised. As countless politicians have reminded us, extraordinary times inspire extraordinary measures.

But it's easy to sneer at such blatant nationalism. What's harder—extraordinary times or not—is to actually do something different, to nurture a classroom experience that is engaging and meaningful to kids, and that doesn't sell out to mainstream blandness. During my years as a middle school teacher, I struggled with that constantly. My efforts to help my students think critically, to provoke them to examine the constraints and possibilities of their lives, were far too sporadic. I'd rock the boat one day, then bail water for the next three.

As a teacher-educator, I still spend a lot of time bailing, but I've discovered that one of my strengths is an ability to empathize—not because of any inherent goodness on my part, but because I've fallen on my face so regularly in my own classrooms. When I talk with my summer students about the kind of teaching I believe in—teaching with a critical edge, with a political consciousness, with cultural relevancy—I never tell them it's easy. I only tell them it's possible. . . .

Waking Teenagers Up

Part of what I try to do in the Diversity class is wake teenagers up a bit, push them to consider ideas they may not have thought about before and, in doing so, clarify their reasons for teaching. This is especially important for white students, many of whom—though certainly not all—come from comfortable suburban subdivisions or two-stoplight towns. While such places are saddled with unfair stereotypes of

their own, the opportunities they provide for whites to interact with people of other races or cultures are often minimal.
Many white students enter the class with cheery attitudes
and good intentions, but they're usually expecting the sort of
rah-rah positiveness associated with superficial gestures toward multiculturalism. Sing a stanza of "We Are the World,"
and be done with it.

A Different Perspective

I can't imagine being in a class where the discussion is on a
particular ethnic group or culture, and there is no one with
in-depth knowledge on the subject present. How can a group
of all-white students have a serious discussion about slavery,
bilingual education, immigration, racism or even affirmative
action without recognizing that they are missing some key
perspectives in the argument?

Without diversified student bodies, many minority students
. . . are forced to be the "official speakers" for their race. As a
black student at a mostly white high school, I've helped my
classmates understand more about the black experience, but I
do get tired of being the "official representative" of my race.

Diversity alleviates the pressure on students like me who often
have to speak as representatives for our entire race just because
we are the only black, Asian or Latino person in the room.

Candace Coleman, *Teaching Tolerance*, June 18, 2003.

One comment I often hear from white students in my Diversity classes goes something like this: "I don't care what
color my students are. Their race doesn't matter. They're all
the same to me." To some prospective teachers, those words
sound not like an expression of naiveté, but like a crystalliza-
tion of why they want to teach in the first place: They love
kids. All kids. That's not only the summation of their bud-
ding philosophies of education—it's the whole thing. Part of
my job is to help them see that, though there's certainly
nothing wrong with loving children, teaching is about a lot
more than just that.

This is not to say I tailor my lessons to white students.
Teenagers of color come in with their own limited experiences, and whether the topic is race, religion, or sexual orientation, it soon becomes clear that bigotry knows no bound-

aries. But as a white person myself—one who has struggled to comprehend both racism and the unearned privileges I've received because of it—I feel an added responsibility to help white students become more aware of their blind spots. In that sense, being a white, middle-class, straight, male instructor has its advantages. I can ask students to confront racism without whites being able to dismiss me as an angry African American or Latino. I can also have them wrestle with homophobia without straight kids thinking I'm doing so out of a personal agenda. In other words, it's harder for those who need to open their eyes to simply turn away. . . .

An Ongoing Process

If students leave my Diversity classes feeling more committed to respecting differences among people, to listening to alternate views, to learning more about other cultures, I won't complain. The world isn't such a kind place sometimes—a fact that was evident even before September 11—and I'm all for any effort that promotes greater understanding. It may sound corny, and educators at both ends of the political spectrum may scoff, but it'd be hard to deny that such empathy is needed.

Of course it's not all that's needed, and that's where efforts that call themselves multicultural often come up short. According to the editors of *Rethinking Schools*, a quarterly journal that focuses on issues affecting urban classrooms, multicultural education should be about much more than nods to diversity and tolerance. "At its best," they write in a recent issue that looks back on the movement's 30 years, "multiculturalism is an ongoing process of questioning, revising, and struggling to create greater equity in every nook and cranny of school life. . . . And it is part of a broader movement to create a more equitable society. It is a fight against racism and other forms of oppression. . . . It is a fight for economic and social justice."

I have no illusions that I achieve such lofty goals with my Diversity classes, but I know that's the kind of education I'm after. Call it multiculturalism, call it teaching for social justice, call it what you want— labels don't matter all that much.

What matters is helping aspiring teachers begin to see

schools as arenas of struggle and to see themselves as people who can bring about change. What matters is helping them understand that there's no such thing as a neutral classroom, that teaching, by its very nature, is a political act. We're all teaching for and against something, whether we choose to acknowledge it or not. Though I doubt they'd ever admit it, those who rant and rave against multiculturalism understand that all too well.

| *"Separate spaces . . . meant that racist biases in educational systems could be countered by wise black teachers."*

Segregation Can Benefit Minorities

bell hooks

Writer and feminist social critic bell hooks argues in the following viewpoint that despite the evils of segregation, in some instances having separate racial spaces has proven beneficial to black people. Within these separate spheres, she asserts, blacks are free to create positive images of themselves and to challenge stereotypes. In segregated spaces, hooks claims, young blacks encounter black role models who doubt their potential. bell hooks is the author of *Salvation: Black People and Love*, from which this viewpoint is taken.

As you read, consider the following questions:

1. How did hooks's mother counter stereotypes of blacks in the media?
2. Why does hooks consider it important for children to be supervised while watching television?
3. How did desegregation have a negative impact on black students, in the author's opinion?

D ecolonization is the necessary groundwork for the development of self-love. It offers us the tools to resist white supremacist thinking. The heart of decolonization is the recognition of equality among humans, coupled with the understanding that racial categories which negatively stigmatize blackness were created as a political tool of imperialist white domination. Most black people first confront white supremacy in the context of blackness, usually through discussion and/or responses to our appearance. Since the logic of white supremacy is that black is always bad and white always good, in order to decolonize, such thinking has to be rejected and replaced by the logic of self-acceptance. Learning to be positive, to affirm ourselves, is a way to cultivate self-love, to intervene on shaming that is racialized.

Significantly, during the worst periods of racial apartheid in the United States, black people were more acutely aware of the need to vigilantly resist internalizing white supremacist thought. Everything was segregated in the world I grew up in. Most white southerners expected black folks to behave in a manner indicating acceptance of subordination. In the presence of whites we were expected to not speak until we were spoken to, to never question anything a white person said, to always allow them preferential treatment, to obey them. The list could go on. Decolonized black people recognized not only that these expectations were unjust but that if we all conformed to them we would be both accepting and perpetuating the notion that it was our destiny to be second-class citizens. No black person could escape working within the constraints imposed on us by white supremacist capitalist patriarchy, but in all ways progressive decolonized black people found the means to resist.

Affirming Black Self-Worth

Segregation meant that in our all black spaces, the institutions which governed our communities—church, school, social club—black folks could fully claim the subjectivity denied us by the larger white world. It was even possible for some clever individuals to live and prosper without really encountering the white power structure. As in the case of those escaped slaves (Maroons, renegades) who became insurgent resisters

creating their own oppositional freedom culture in hidden locations, powerful individuals in our all-black communities
were able to offer us liberatory ways to think about blackness.
When we were growing up, my mother and father were careful to create an environment in our home where racial stereotypes were always challenged. My mother came from a family where her mother could pass for white and her father was
very dark. Acutely sensitive to the conflicts color caste systems create, she was determined to raise her family in an environment where all would be regarded equally. This was important because our large family, like her family of origin, was
made up of individuals with various shades and hues. Whenever anything appeared in the mass media that was negative
and stereotypical about blackness, our mother would counter
this information with constant affirmation of our worth and
value as black people. I remember watching beauty pageants
with Mama where all the contestants were white. She would
say, "Look at them, they are nowhere near as beautiful or tal-
ented as you are." Or if she approved of a white female, she
urged me to use this example to better myself.

Without knowing fancy political terms like "decolonization," our mother intuitively understood that consciously
working to instill positive self-esteem in black children was
an utter necessity. Her values were reinforced by all the black
institutions in our community. Ironically, at that time everyone viewed the lack of black representation in mass media as
a mark of racial injustice and white supremacist domination,
but in retrospect our self-esteem as black people was stronger
then than it is now because we were not constantly bombarded by dehumanizing images of ourselves. When we
watched shows like *Tarzan* or *Amos 'n' Andy* that we enjoyed,
we were ever aware that the images of blackness we saw on
these programs were created by folks who, as Mama would
say, "did not like us." Consequently, these images had to be
viewed with a critical eye.

The Need for New Strategies

In my own family this critical vigilance began to change as the
fruits of the civil rights struggle became more apparent.
Mama's last child would watch television alone with no adult

voices teaching her a resisting gaze. By the end of the sixties many black people felt they could sit back, relax, and exercise their full rights as citizens of this free nation. Once laws desegregated the country, new strategies had to be developed to keep black folks from equality, to keep black folks in place. While emerging as less racist than it had once been, television became the new vehicle for racist propaganda. Black people could be represented in negative ways, but those who had wanted there to be jobs for black actors could be appeased. Nothing pushed the lessons of a white supremacist aesthetic more than television, a medium where even dark-haired white women had to become blondes in order to succeed.

A Strange Transition for Wynton Marsalis

From the kindergarten to third grade, I went to an all black school. So then I was like, everybody liked me. I was the funny guy, I cracked all the jokes. It was different because we were all the same. And then from the fourth grade to seventh grade, I went to an all white school, except there were two or three black kids, so that was totally different. So as in the black school, everybody liked you, if you made good grades they said you were smart, in the white school, you were like the enemy or something. . . . It was just a very strange transition to me, in terms of school. Because at the one end, if you were doing good, you were elevated, you were given credit. At the other, you always had a battle on your hands.

"Interview: Wynton Marsalis," Academy of Achievement Web site, January 8, 1991. www.achievement.org.

Since television has primarily exploited stereotypical images of blackness, small children held captive by these screen images from birth on absorb the message that black is inferior, unworthy, dumb, evil, and criminal. While well-meaning black parents attempt to counteract the racism of the culture by affirming blackness in their homes, their efforts are easily undermined by mass media. When black children are allowed to watch television unsupervised, white supremacist attitudes are taught them even before they reach grade school. It was easier for black folks to create positive images of ourselves when we were not daily bombarded by negative screen images. This may explain why individual black people came through the terrible period of racial apartheid with much better self-concepts than those of many young black people born when racial integration was more an accepted norm.

When there was no racial integration, black people were more vigilant about safeguarding the integrity of our lives in the midst of ongoing racist assault. Separate spaces also meant that racist biases in educational systems could be countered by wise black teachers. Those who attended all-black schools in the years before the militant black power struggle, institutions named for important black leaders (Crispus Attucks, Booker T. Washington, George Washington Carver, et al.), were educated in a world where we were valued. While we studied the same lessons that were studied in the white schools, our teachers added lessons in black history and culture. Since everyone in the school system was black, we had perfect role models. No one doubted our ability to learn, to excel academically.

Well-Meaning Bias

When our black schools were closed down and we were forced to integrate predominately white schools situated far away from our neighborhoods, it caused tremendous psychological depression. Regarded as first-class citizens in our beloved schools, we were now bussed to schools where we were treated as second-class citizens, where white teachers saw us as inferior, as savages, incapable of being their equals. When a black student excelled academically, they were regarded as the grand exception to the rule and treated by whites as a Negro pet. No psychologists or school counselors stood in the wings (nor do they stand there today) to help black children cope with the reality of moving from segregated schools where we had been valued to white schools where our teachers saw us only as a problem, where a great many of them actually hated us.

Few black people had foreseen that equal access to educational institutions would not have a positive impact if within those newly integrated classrooms black pupils would be taught by teachers perpetuating racist stereotypes, who encouraged us to feel shame and hatred for our race. Often the most well-meaning white teachers still held racist attitudes, which they expressed openly. When my well-meaning, supportive white female drama teacher told me no black man would ever love me because I was "too smart," she did not see herself as perpetuating a racist stereotype about black males. Once we left our all-black schools, gifted black male students "disappeared." They had always been visible in our all-black schools. At home our parents talked about this unfair treatment of black males; racist white folks simply did not want gifted white girls sitting next to black boys.

Failing Black Students

No one attended to the psychological needs of those boys who had once been recognized as gifted but were suddenly forced to go backward. One of the smartest black boys in my peer group had a breakdown shortly after graduation. Yet for the most part all these psychological traumas went unnoticed and the psychological pain they created went untreated. When we showed signs of psychological disturbance in our homes, fear of attending school when we had once loved our classes, we were encouraged to accept the pain as part of the civil rights struggle. Our mission was to endure the indignities inflicted upon us to uplift the race. Still, this did not, and does not, mean that we were not wounded by the process.

Detecting Racial Bias

Placing our education in the hands of unenlightened educators has always been dangerous and still is. Racist biases often shape both the information black students receive in schools and the manner in which they are treated when they seek empowerment by striving to excel academically. In their book *The Power of Soul*, Darlene and Derek Hopson tell this story: "When Derek was entering high school, he wanted to take college preparatory courses, yet despite his previously good grades, a white guidance counselor discouraged him from taking on such a challenge. Instead, the counselor advised Derek that he 'do something with his hands so he wouldn't be frustrated,' meaning that he pursue vocational or technical training rather than academics." As a loving advocate for her grandson, Derek's grandmother went to his school and intervened, helping him to forge ahead. African-

American oral history is full of such narratives. Currently, many white teachers may be kind to black students and still direct them away from striving for academic excellence. This kindness often has led parental caregivers and students to let down their guard and not be as vigilant in detecting racial biases when they emerge from well-meaning souls.

"More than forty-five years after the landmark U.S. Supreme Court Brown v. Board of Education *decision, school segregation in the United States persists."*

School Segregation Is a Serious Problem

Beverly Daniel Tatum

In the following viewpoint Beverly Daniel Tatum argues that forty-five years after the Supreme Court mandated desegregation, racial segregation in America's schools persists. In some cases, she maintains, segregation occurs because African American and Latino students attend schools primarily in poor communities while white students attend schools in middle-class neighborhoods. This separation, Tatum contends, prevents progress toward racial equality, which can only be achieved if students connect across racial lines. Tatum is president of Spelman College.

As you read, consider the following questions:

1. According to Tatum, what steps will interrupt self-segregation?
2. Why is mutual engagement important, in the author's opinion?
3. In the study cited by the author, what percentage of students described their groups of friends as racially and ethnically diverse?

More than forty-five years after the landmark U.S. Supreme Court *Brown v. Board of Education* decision, school segregation in the United States persists. In fact, it has been on the rise since the early 1990s. There is a strong relationship between racial segregation and concentrated poverty. National data show that most segregated African American and Latino schools are dominated by poor children, but that 96 percent of White schools have middle-class majorities. Such segregation cuts children of color off from educational and employment networks of opportunity.

Dismantling Systems of Oppression

Segregation and inequality are strongly self-perpetuating, yet the ideal of democratic education is to create an environment in which such patterns can be interrupted. The first step in interrupting this cycle of inequity is mutual engagement. We will not be able to effectively dismantle systems of oppression—systems of inequity—without working in coalition with one another across lines of difference. Yet because of persistent residential and school segregation, the opportunities young people in the United States have had to interact with those racially, ethnically, or religiously different from them have typically been quite limited. This lack of direct experience means that what one learns about the "other" is based on secondhand information, information too often conveyed in the form of media stereotypes or parental prejudices. Exactly who the "other" is varies, depending on where students have grown up and what their life experience has been. But we can be sure that all members of our campus populations have come to college with stereotypes and prejudices about other segments of the student body. Such preconception is unavoidable when there is so much misinformation circulating. And these biases are a barrier to meaningful engagement across lines of difference.

Why does engagement matter? It should be clear that diversity is not the end in itself. It is not *just* about being friends. It *is* about being allies and becoming effective agents of change. To work effectively as an agent of change in a pluralistic society, it is necessary to be able to connect with people different from oneself. Most students do not come with this capacity for connection already developed, yet it is a capacity that can be developed. In the context of the self-perpetuating nature of inequity, meaningful engagement is an important step, a prerequisite for the transformative education we need for a more just society.

An Integration Time Line

1849 The Massachusetts Supreme Court rules that segregated schools are permissible under the state's constitution in *Roberts v. City of Boston.*

1896 The Supreme Court authorizes segregation in *Plessy v. Ferguson*, finding Louisiana's "separate but equal" law constitutional.

1954 In a unanimous opinion, the Supreme Court in *Brown v. Board of Education* overturns *Plessy* and declares that separate schools are "inherently unequal."

1957 More than 1,000 paratroopers from the 101st Airborne Division and a federalized Arkansas National Guard protect nine black students integrating Central High School in Little Rock, Ark.

1959 Prince Edward County, Va., officials close their public schools rather than integrate them.

1971 The Court approves mandated busing in *Swann v. Charlotte-Mecklenburg Board of Education.*

1988 School integration reaches its all-time high; almost 45% of black students in the United States are attending majority-white schools.

2003 A study by Harvard's Civil Rights Project finds that schools were more segregated in 2000 than in 1970 when busing for desegregation began.

Jennifer Holladay, *Teaching Tolerance*, Spring 2004.

Increasingly, faculty, students, and administrators alike are recognizing the importance of engagement across difference as an essential dimension of preparing the next generation for effective participation in a pluralistic world. This focus on diversity is supported by a growing body of empirical research demonstrating the educational benefit of learning in a diverse community. After analyzing national data drawn from nearly 200 colleges and universities as well as data specific to the University of Michigan, social psychologist Patricia Gurin concluded that students who experienced the most racial and ethnic diversity in and out of their classrooms benefited most in terms of both "learning outcomes" and "democracy outcomes." In learning outcomes, these students showed the greatest engagement in active thinking processes, growth in intellectual engagement and motivation, and growth in intellectual and academic skills. In democracy outcomes, they showed the most engagement during college in various forms of citizenship and the most involvement with people from different races and cultures, and they were the most likely to acknowledge that group differences are compatible with the interests of the broader community. These results persisted beyond graduation. Students with the most diversity experiences during college had the most cross-racial friends, neighbors, and work associates nine years after they entered college.

The benefits of engaging diversity are compelling, but are enough students taking advantage of these formal and informal learning opportunities? Are students learning to negotiate across lines of difference, lines defined not only by race but also by class, ethnicity, gender, sexual orientation, or religion? Or are they still building their own homogeneous networks, operating in circles that rarely intersect, and failing to engage meaningfully with those whose backgrounds differ from their own?

The Problem of Self-Segregation
The popular perception is that the latter situation is more common, particularly in reference to race. Newspapers and magazines regularly feature stories about the dilemma of so-called self-segregation on college campuses. . . . Despite this perception, there is some evidence that students desire more cross-group interaction than a quick glance at the cafeteria may indicate.

In a recent study of friendship groups within a diverse campus community, researcher Anthony Lising Antonio found that more than 90 percent of the 638 third-year students he surveyed reported that students predominantly cluster by race and ethnicity, but almost half (46 percent) described their own friendship groups as racially and ethnically mixed. Clearly, these students did not view their behavior as the norm. They still perceived segregation as the rule, a perception reinforced by the fact that African American students were the most likely to report racially or ethnically homogeneous friendship groups and one in three White students also reported having racially homogeneous friendship groups. The pattern of social isolation of both Black and White students is a visible symbol of the continuing legacy of past and present systems of inequity.

This pattern is also an expression of different goals for interracial contact. In a study of Berkeley undergraduates, Troy Duster and his associates found that most students express interest in more interracial experiences, yet how that interest is engaged varies along racial lines. White students wanted to make friends with African Americans, but they wanted to do so in informal settings, and were less likely to want to participate in special programs, courses, or activities that structure interethnic contacts. In contrast, African Americans were far more likely to want special programs and activities and were less interested in developing cross-racial friendships and social activities. Both groups wanted interracial experiences but on different terms. Duster concluded, "The task is to provide all students with a range of safe environments and options where they can explore and develop terms that they find comfortable. In the absence of such opportunities, the tendencies remain for each group to see the others from a distance, in terms of images, stereotypes, stories, and myths that are not informed by direct contact and experience."

We know, empirically and experientially, that the challenge of educating a diverse student body that will be ready to live and work together in an increasingly complex and pluralistic society requires us to interrupt patterns of social isolation. We must provide opportunities for students to practice, opportunities to understand multiple perspectives as well as individual ones during the college years.

Periodical Bibliography

The following articles have been selected to supplement the diverse views presented in this chapter.

Ricardo Alonso-Zaldivar — "What's in a Racial Identity?" *Los Angeles Times*, December 9, 2004.

Ignatius Bau and Shilpa Patel — "Melting Pot or Not: The Evolving Multiracial Face of America," *Asian Week*, November 1–7, 2002.

Amitai Etzioni — "A New American Race?" *Responsive Community*, Spring 2000.

Abdon Ibarra — "'Hispanic' Label a Creation of Politicians," *Lexington Herald-Tribune*, May 27, 2004.

Shavar D. Jeffries — "What's Wrong with California's Racial Privacy Initiative?" *CNN.com Law Center*, September 5, 2002. http://archives.cnn.com/2002/LAW/09/columns/jeffries.racial.privacy.09.05.

Elan Journo — "Multiculturalism's War on Education," *Bucks County Courier Times*, September 26, 2004.

Martin Kasindorf and Haya El Nasser — "Impact of Census' Race Data Debated," *USA Today*, March 12, 2001.

Jerry Lange — "Hispanics and Racial Identity," *Seattle Times*, December 9, 2004.

Leonard Pitts — "A Colorblind America Isn't Possible, or Even Desirable," *Milwaukee Journal Sentinel*, July 20, 2002.

Dinesh Ramde — "Race Holds Little Importance in Biology, Genetics," *Daily Cardinal*, April 19, 2004.

Edward G. Rozycki — "Multiculturalism and the Problems of Immigration," *Educational Horizons*, Winter 2000.

Warren St. John — "Greens in Black and White," *New York Times*, October 6, 2004.

Erin Texeira — "Term Minority Criticized as Outdated," *Washington Post*, August 18, 2005.

CHAPTER 2

What Impact Does Immigration Have on Interracial America?

Chapter Preface

A Latino family in a Chicago suburb is awoken at 4:50 A.M. by nine building inspectors and police officers who prohibit the family from getting dressed or moving about while the officials search the entire house to find evidence of overcrowding. A Muslim imam, an elder and prayer leader, from the Dallas area is arrested by police upon leaving a mosque after an outreach event. Officers search his vehicle, arrest him for expired vehicle tags, and confiscate his computer. While racial profiling can affect people of all races and nationalities, it is a particular concern among immigrants in the United States. Since the terrorist attacks of September 11, 2001, national security concerns have made some feel that racial profiling is justified; however, others worry that the practice is neither helpful nor just. This controversy is one of many in the debate over the impact of immigration and race relations in America.

Some commentators feel that the only way to effectively combat terrorism is to consider as a factor the race, ethnicity, and nationality of potential perpetrators. These analysts argue that taking this information into account may prevent further attacks. Chief Deputy Attorney General for the State of California Peter Siggins claims, "The mission of responsible law enforcement officials in combating domestic terrorism is to take what they know to be true about the ethnic identity of the September 11th assailants, and combine it with other factors developed through investigation and analysis to focus investigative efforts and avoid casting a net too wide." While Siggins acknowledges that race cannot be the only factor in finding potential terrorists, he also asserts, "Perhaps there is a need to adjust our expectations in a time of national emergency."

Opponents of using racial profiling to identify potential terrorists are concerned that infringing upon civil liberties in this way is fundamentally unjust. They contend that justice should be color-blind and that using race as a factor in determining who may or may not be a criminal constitutes racial prejudice. Edward Barocas, legal director for the American Civil Liberties Union of New Jersey claims,

"Racial profiling violates our Constitution's promise of equal protection and the right to be presumed innocent." Racial profiling can also be counterproductive, they argue, and in fact leads officials to discount real threats to our national security. "It's not just a bad thing, it's ineffective," says Ed Yohnka, director of communications for the American Civil Liberties Union of Illinois. "It's distracting from the real work that police ought to be doing. And it divides communities—the divisions created post-9/11 between Muslim and Southeast Asian communities and the police are very disturbing. It creates a kind of fear and anxiety in communities that doesn't serve any of us very well," Yohnka maintains.

In June 2003 the Department of Justice issued its Guidance Regarding the Use of Race by Federal Law Enforcement Agencies, which forbids racial profiling by federal law enforcement officials. However, the guidance does not cover profiling based on religion, religious appearance, or national origin. It also contains a blanket exception for "national security" and "border integrity" cases. The human rights group Amnesty International has expressed concern that these exceptions, along with flimsy enforcement of these rules, could allow racial profiling to continue, and immigrants, they claim, will continue to be unjustly targeted.

The debate about racial profiling, which has simmered in the United States for many years, has been given new life since the terrorist attacks of September 11, 2001. The controversy highlights not just issues concerning race but immigration as well. In the following chapter the authors examine how race and immigration intersect in increasingly complex ways since the September 11 attacks.

"[A] terrorist infrastructure is being created, and it grows with each wave of unassimilated immigrants from Mexico."

Mexican Immigrants Threaten American Unity

William Norman Grigg

Immigration from Mexico shows no sign of slowing, argues William Norman Grigg in the following viewpoint. In fact, he maintains, Mexican immigrants threaten to take over the United States through both overt terrorist action and subtle cultural reoccupation. As the border between the two countries dissolves, Grigg claims, the risk of terrorism from unassimilated Mexican immigrants, who dream of taking back land that once belonged to Mexico, increases. Grigg is senior editor of the *New American*, a conservative newsmagazine.

As you read, consider the following questions:
1. According to Grigg, how many Mexicans will have entered the United States during the tenure of Mexican president Vicente Fox?
2. In the author's view, what other country faced a similar problem with ethnic separatism?
3. How does the author define a matricular card?

William Norman Grigg, "Aztlan and Amalgamation," *The New American*, May 6, 2002. Copyright © 2002 by American Opinion Publishing, Inc. Reproduced by permission.

While American troops engage al-Qaeda terrorist cells in far-flung battlefields across Asia and our military leadership prepares for a Gulf War encore against Iraq, our "friend" and "neighbor" to the South is relentlessly invading our homeland. The Mexican government and radical "Chicano" groups in this country are pursuing the dream of La Reconquista—the "re-conquest" of the southwestern United States.

The Reoccupation

"More than a century after the U.S. invasion of Mexico that resulted in the annexation of Texas, Mexicans are 'reoccupying' the territory, but through less violent means and for different reasons," reported Monica Mendel of TheNewsMexico.com news service on March 25, [2002]. "Most of these immigrants live in border states like California, Texas, Arizona, and New Mexico, the same ones Mexico lost when President Antonio Lopez de Santa Anna signed an agreement to end the U.S. invasion in 1848 by ceding 2.5 million square kilometers of Mexican territory to the United States."

The provocative term "reoccupation" was not coined by an anti-immigration activist. Rather, it was used in an official study published by the Mexican government's National Council on Population (Conapo). Mendel writes: "The 'reoccupation' of this territory has been slow but steady, and the number of immigrants is growing every year." Citing Conapo's findings, Mendel predicts that during the six-year reign of incumbent Mexican President Vicente Fox, ending in 2006, "two million Mexicans will enter the United States at the rate of approximately 380,000 per year.". . .

Aztlan

Charles Truxillo, a professor of "Chicano Studies" at the University of New Mexico, believes that Los Angeles will one day be the capital of "La Republica del Norte"—a Hispanic nation straddling the border between the southwest United States and northern Mexico. The envisioned "Chicano homeland" would absorb the existing U.S. states of California, Arizona, New Mexico, and Texas, and southern Colorado, as well as "the northern tier of current Mexican states:

Baja California, Sonora, Chihuahua, Coahuila, Nuevo Leon and Tamaulipas," reported the March 10, [2002] *Albuquerque News.*

The envisioned "Chicano homeland" is also referred to as "Aztlan." The geographical boundaries for the proposed homeland have not been precisely defined; in addition to the U.S. states cited by the *Albuquerque News*, Nevada and Utah have also been mentioned.

The new polity won't appear "within the next 20 years but within 80 years," predicts Truxillo. "I may not live to see the Hispanic homeland, but by the end of the century my students will live in it, sovereign and free." While Truxillo maintains that the new country should be created "by any means necessary," he insists that it is "unlikely" that it will be born out of a civil war. Instead, he foresees that "La Republica del Norte" will be created "by political process, by the 'electoral pressure' of the future majority Hispanic population," observes the *Albuquerque News.*

Terrorist Subcurrents

What does Truxillo mean when he invokes the familiar revolutionary refrain, "By any means necessary"? One clue can be found in how Truxillo reveres Reies Lopez Tijerina, a bloody-handed 1960s Chicano agitator. It was from Tijerina, states Truxillo, that he learned "I was a member of a people with a country that had been taken from them by war, a land that was our own by treaty."

Tijerina's chief claim to infamy was his role in leading a June 1967 guerrilla assault on the courthouse in Tierra Amarilla, New Mexico. During the two-hour assault, Tijerina and 150 terrorist thugs killed Deputy Sheriff Nicainor Saizan, pistol-whipped Undersheriff Dan Rivera, and shot 63-year-old jailer Eugolio Salazar. The Tijerina-led mob also took 20 local citizens hostage in the courthouse before fleeing town. Although Salazar survived the initial assault, he was beaten to death before he could testify at Tijerina's trial. With the jury and material witnesses intimidated by the possibility of another outbreak of violence, Tijerina—who had shot Salazar pointblank in the face—was given a two-year sentence, of which he served six months before being paroled.

Immigrants in the United States

Illegal immigrants account for almost 30 percent of the U.S. foreign-born population. More than half of all illegal immigrants are from Mexico.

Status of foreign-born population
As of March 2004

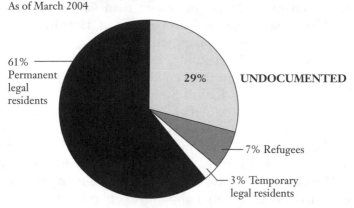

61% Permanent legal residents

29% UNDOCUMENTED

7% Refugees

3% Temporary legal residents

Origin of illegal immigrants

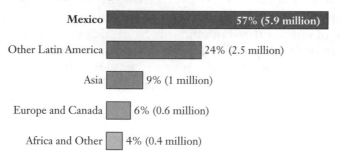

Mexico 57% (5.9 million)

Other Latin America 24% (2.5 million)

Asia 9% (1 million)

Europe and Canada 6% (0.6 million)

Africa and Other 4% (0.4 million)

Sylvia Moreno, Pew Hispanic Center, cited in the *Washington Post*, March 22, 2005.

In a "Manifesto" published in the *Albuquerque Journal* shortly before the attack on Tierra Amarilla, Tijerina's terrorist group laid claim to millions of acres of the American Southwest—including the states of California, Arizona, and New Mexico—on behalf of the "Nation of Aztlan." Tijerina and his thugs asserted "exclusive and supreme" powers "within our territorial jurisdiction, over all persons and property situated therein, to the exclusion of all other countries and governments.". . .

"¡Viva la Revolución!"

After descending into obscurity, Tijerina dramatically reappeared at the national "Latino Leadership Summit" at the University of California-Riverside in January 1995. Introduced to an audience of radical professors, lawyers, labor leaders, student agitators, and more than 400 "Latino activists," Tijerina was greeted with sustained, tumultuous applause. Many in the crowd raised their right arms in the communist clenched-fist salute, exclaiming "¡Viva la Revolución!" and "Power to the People!"

Present at the 1995 Latino Summit were representatives of the "Brown Berets de Aztlan," a paramilitary group that threatened to "make the streets run red" with their opponent's blood. Also prominent were representatives of the Movimiento Estudiantil Chicano de Aztlan (Chicano Student Movement of Aztlan, or MEChA), a militant separatist group active on high school and university campuses. . . .

Do MEChA and its Aztlandista allies have the means to match their ambitions? Not yet, obviously. But their terrorist infrastructure is being created, and it grows with each wave of unassimilated immigrants from Mexico. Kosovo offers an ominous parallel: The narco-terrorist Kosovo Liberation Army (KLA), which now governs that Serbian province under UN supervision, recruited much of its membership through campus-based ethnic separatism among ethnic Albanians. And the KLA's campaign to seize Kosovo gained strength through rampant illegal immigration from Serbia's southern neighbor, Albania.

Assimilation in Reverse

Historically, immigrants to the United States were expected to assimilate our language, customs, and public culture. However, as the border between the United States and Mexico erodes, we are witnessing what could be called "assimilation in reverse" as the public institutions of the affected communities are required to accommodate large, undigested masses of Mexicans.

For example: The City of Houston has announced that the "matricular card," a form of identification issued by the Mexican Consulate, would be "considered official identification by Houston police officers," reported the March 8, [2002] *Houston Chronicle*. The paper notes that this is a particularly welcome development for Mexicans whose "immigration status may be in question . . . [and therefore] have no valid U.S. forms of identification, such as a driver's license."

All that is required to obtain a matricular card, noted a March 22, [2002] Fox News report, is "a Mexican birth certificate and some proof of U.S. residency." No proof of U.S. citizenship is required. In some states, continued the Fox News report, "matricular ID holders can use the card as one of two pieces of identification needed to apply for a driver's license.". . .

The Border Vanishes

The Mexican government, radical Chicano separatists, and the Bush administration all agree on one thing: The border separating our nation from Mexico should be treated as if it does not exist. The Fox regime, like previous Mexican governments for decades, uses its porous northern border as a safety valve, exporting its unemployable citizens and then organizing them within our nation as a potent political bloc. Chicano separatists intoxicated with dreams of a new "homeland" radicalize young, poorly assimilated Mexicans for a street-level army that may prove a larger long-term threat than Osama bin Laden's al-Qaeda terrorist network. And the Bush administration, pursuing a plan for continental "integration," treats Mexico as if it were already part of a consolidated political unit with the United States.

In his new book *Warrior Politics*, journalist Robert D. Kaplan correctly points out that "the tumultuous historic consolidation of Mexico and the United States" is just one facet of a process of "global political convergence" into a "kind of loose world governance. . . ."

As "these two vastly unequal societies [the United States and Mexico] integrate at breakneck speed," the immediate result will be "social upheaval on both sides of the border." But from the perspective of the globalist elite—a view that Kaplan enthusiastically shares—this is simply the price that must be paid to bring about a unified world.

"Studies demonstrate that Mexican Americans support American core values at least as much as Anglos."

Mexican Immigrants Do Not Threaten American Unity

League of United Latin American Citizens and Mexican American Legal Defense and Educational Fund

In the following viewpoint the League of United Latin American Citizens and Mexican American Legal Defense and Educational Fund refute allegations that immigrants from Mexico are threatening American culture. On the contrary, they assert, Latinos have made great contributions to the United States. Latino soldiers, they maintain for example, have won many medals for service in the U.S. military, and Mexican immigrants have contributed billions to the U.S. economy. Mexico and the United States have had a long, intertwined history, and Americans should see Mexican immigrants not as a threat, but as an asset, the authors assert.

As you read, consider the following questions:

1. In the authors' opinion, what percentage of Latina/ Latino children report that their parents want them to go to college?
2. According to the authors, when did the United States acquire from Mexico the states currently known as the Southwest?
3. Until what year do the authors write that it was legal to enter the United States without the U.S. government's permission?

League of United Latin American Citizens and Mexican American Legal Defense and Educational Fund, "Joint Statement of MALDEF and LULAC," www. maldef.org, April 23, 2004. Reproduced by permission.

The United States is a nation of immigrants from around the world. In the U.S., individual accomplishment is valued. The very foundation of American democracy is the Bill of Rights, respecting and even guaranteeing individual rights.

By passing various civil rights laws in the 1960's, Congress re-established that our Constitution also means that not one race, religion or ethnicity should dominate another. The American dream is built upon the hard work of immigrants and the fundamental value of equal opportunity.

We must not go back to a system where one's race, class or religion determines one's fate, regardless of one's intellect or willingness to work hard. [Samuel] Huntington [in his book *Who Are We? The Challenges to America's National Identity*] has made astonishing and unsupported generalizations about Latinos. His generalizations about Latinos being "persistent" in immigrating to the U.S., being exceedingly fertile, having less interest in education and not wanting to learn English are not based on fact and appear to emanate from a prejudice against Latinos. He has no proof that every Latino/a, or even the majority of Latinos/as and their families, fall into these stereotypes, nor any proof that Latinos are very different from other ethnic groups.

This kind of analysis harkens back to the justifications for legal segregation and discriminatory policies that were commonplace prior to the civil rights laws of the 1960's. Mexican Americans and Latino immigrants are not inferior to white Anglo-Protestants.

Latino Values

A . . . *New York Times* poll found that Latino immigrants are hard-working, have strong family values, do not take public benefits, and generally epitomize the American dream. Latino immigrants are contributing billions of dollars to the economy and even creating jobs for U.S. citizens. Studies consistently find that immigrants contribute far more in taxes to the government than they use in government services. Latina/o parents value education and encourage their children to do well in school at the same rates as Anglo parents, with more than 90 percent of Latina/o children reporting that their parents want them to go to college. Moreover, studies demonstrate that Mexican Americans support American core values at least as much as Anglos. Huntington alleges that Latinos do not want to become American, despite the fact that Latino immigrants consciously choose to leave their home countries and migrate to the U.S. in order to become American and live the American dream, especially for their children.

Everything that is traditionally thought of as "American," Latinos live out fully. They are family-oriented, religious, hard-working and loyal to the U.S. In fact, Latinos have won more medals of honor for their service in the U.S. military than any other ethnic group.

Succeeding Despite Barriers

Huntington fails to take into account that the significant accomplishments of Latinos have occurred in spite of the long and shameful history of discrimination specifically directed against Latinos in the U.S. When Huntington alleges that Latinos have not achieved as much as whites in education, he neglects to acknowledge the history of segregation against Latinos, and Mexican Americans in particular, especially in the Southwest. Even today, when legal segregation is outlawed, Huntington does not take into account that Latinos are attending the most segregated schools in the country, which are providing a lesser quality of education as compared to majority white schools. Predominantly minority schools have less-qualified teachers, more overcrowding, worse educational facilities, and less access to advanced curricula.

Despite all these barriers, children of Latino immigrants are succeeding at a very high rate. It is ironic that Huntington blames Latinos for segregation. Latinos and other people of color know from tough experience that such segregation is not voluntary, as it is still difficult for Latinos to gain equality in white communities, and there is still discrimination in jobs and housing. However, like African Americans, Latinos have been segregated and mythologized as "different," and subject to unfair criticism, because of their ethnicity.

Huntington criticizes Latinos' use of Spanish and falsely alleges that Latinos do not want to learn English. The major-

An English Language Learning Curve

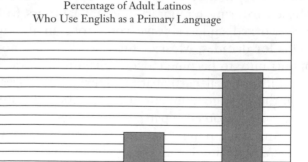

Percentage of Adult Latinos
Who Use English as a Primary Language

American Immigration Law Foundation, "Immigrant Success or Stagnation: Confronting the Claim of Latino Non-Advancement," 2003.

ity of Latinos speak English. Among Spanish-speaking Latinos, poll after poll shows that Latinos want to learn English. Their ability to learn English is sometimes limited if they entered the U.S. at an older age and when they do not have access to English classes because they are working more than one job and there are limited English classes offered.

A Unique Historical Relationship

As far as the ability to speak Spanish, Huntington portrays it as a negative, whereas in the global economy, many see such language capabilities are a positive. Huntington mischaracterizes the history between the U.S. and Mexico and the causes for migration patterns between the two countries. Huntington characterizes Mexican immigration as "persistent" and a "massive influx" post-1960's civil rights laws. This characterization fails to recognize the unique, historical relationship between the two countries.

In 1848, the U.S. acquired a significant portion of Mexico, which became what is now known as the Southwest in the U.S. Those people living in that region were Mexican citizens prior to the acquisition. When the U.S. experienced severe labor shortages while its soldiers were fighting in the world wars, the U.S. entered into several agreements with Mexico to bring temporary migrant laborers from Mexico who worked under abusive conditions in the agricultural fields for decades. Most of these workers did not have the opportunity to become citizens, making it difficult to exercise full political participation. During the Great Depression, the U.S. government and a number of state and local governments forced repatriation of one-third of the Mexican American population to impoverished conditions in Mexico. Shockingly, most of those who were deported were U.S. citizens who happened to be of Mexican ethnicity. Despite this checkered past, Mexican immigrants continued to come to the U.S. to fill U.S. economic needs and to pursue economic opportunities not available in Mexico.

Characterizing past non-Mexican immigration as "legal" and current Mexican immigration as "illegal" is false and misleading. Prior to 1939, it was not illegal to enter the U.S. without the U.S. government's permission. Millions of immigrants, mostly from Western Europe, entered the U.S. without proper visas. Currently, many Mexicans enter the U.S. legally. The U.S. legal immigration system, however, is in need of serious overhaul. The current system is not meeting the economic or family reunification principles it was designed to meet. The backlogs in legal visa processing for the spouses and children of Mexican legal immigrants living in the U.S. are causing families to be separated for 13 years. In order to reunite with their families, some Mexican citizens do enter without proper documentation. Present high levels of migration between the U.S. and Mexico are based on geographic proximity and economic interdependence of the two countries. Many Mexicans come here because Mexico is our close neighbor and trading partner. Mexico is closer than Europe so the voyage to America is more natural. The U.S. and Mexican fate and economies are inextricably intertwined. That is, the U.S. is just as dependent on Mexico and Mexican migration as the opposite is true.

"If students are placed in 'English immersion' classes large chunks of the curriculum will be incomprehensible. This violates a basic civil right."

Bilingual Education Protects Immigrants' Civil Rights

Rethinking Schools

In the following viewpoint the editors of *Rethinking Schools*, an activist publication that promotes equal opportunity education, claims that bilingual education is both a civil and a human right. The United Nations, the authors contend, has declared that all children have the right to be educated in their native language. Nevertheless, unwarranted fears of non-English speaking immigrants have led to English-only education initiatives in the United States, the authors assert. Unfortunately, children placed in English-only classrooms do not understand what is being taught, the authors argue, and their education inevitably suffers.

As you read, consider the following questions:

1. According to the authors, what states have policies curtailing bilingual education?
2. Within how many years of entering the U.S. school system does the ESEA require immigrants to take standardized tests in English, according to the authors?
3. What restrictions did California's Proposition 187 initially place on children of undocumented immigrants, in the authors' view?

In 1864, Congress prohibited Native-American children from being taught in their own languages. It took the U.S. government 70 years to overturn that law. Now they're at it again. The federal government and the states have taken steps toward banning bilingual education in several states and weakening it in virtually every state. We hope it won't take another 70 years to restore students' right to learn their own languages in school.

Silicon Valley millionaire Ron Unz has spearheaded four statewide ballot initiatives to ban bilingual education. Three of these have won and resulted in anti-child policies in California (1998), Arizona (2000), and now Massachusetts (2002). In this latest election in Massachusetts, 70 percent of the voters approved the "English for the Children" initiative, which will take bilingual education away from children who need it. (Ironically, Massachusetts was the first state in the nation to legislatively support bilingual education some 31 years ago.)

In Colorado, voters defeated a similar measure (56 percent to 44 percent) [in November 2002], thanks to the hard work of bilingual education activists such as members of English Plus and the financial support of Pat Stryker, a wealthy parent whose child attends a two-way bilingual program in Fort Collins. But such state referenda are just the tip of the iceberg. The federal Elementary and Secondary Education Act (ESEA) includes significant anti-bilingual components that threaten bilingual students in all states.

Emphasizing English

The ESEA requires English Language Learners to take standardized tests in English within three years of entering the U.S. school system—not enough time to gain academic English proficiency. This time crunch forces many bilingual schools to restructure their programs and emphasize English over native-language instruction. The mean-spirited way many states have decided to implement these assessment regimes makes them partners in the federal government's attack on bilingual education. (See www.rethinkingschools.org for background articles.)

James Crawford, one of the nation's best-known writers on bilingual education, wrote in the Summer 2002 issue of

Rethinking Schools that the ESEA was an "Obituary for the Bilingual Education Act of 1968." He explained that a provision of the ESEA eliminated the Bilingual Education Act and replaced it with the English Language Acquisition Act. Where the former stressed language development in both English and students' native languages and promoted equal access to the curriculum, the latter expects schools to focus on English only. And if these attacks weren't enough, "English Only" groups continue to organize to have cities, counties, and states proclaim English as their "official language." Such proposals build on public anti-immigrant sentiment and lead to divisive and unnecessary conflicts.

Xenophobic Policies

It's no coincidence that all of this is occurring during the largest wave of non-English speaking immigrants in the history of the United States. The current xenophobic policies in our schools and communities are the newest chapter in a long, predictable book. (Previous chapters included, among other embarrassments, the outlawing of Native-American languages in schools in 1864 and a rash of shutting down German bilingual education programs in the Midwest during a surge of "nativism" around the time of World War I.)

Many mark the beginning of this new anti-immigrant organizing with the 1994 passage of California's Proposition 187, which made it illegal for children of undocumented immigrants to attend public schools. (Fortunately the Federal Courts ruled this law unconstitutional.) And Unz has since successfully dismantled bilingual ed in California, Arizona, and Massachusetts. Bush took the same side, using federal legislation to weaken bilingual education in those states that Unz has not yet conquered.

A Human and Civil Right

The current attack on bilingual education denies children a basic human and civil right—the right to learn in their native language. Article 29 of the Convention on the Rights of a Child adopted by the General Assembly of the United Nations in 1989 (and ratified by all nations except the United States and Somalia) states that "the education of the child should be directed to . . . the development of respect for the child's parents, his or her own cultural identity, language and values." Article 30 states that "a child belonging to an [ethnic, religious, or linguistic minority] should not be denied the right . . . to use his or her own language."

Kirk. © 1996 by Kirk Anderson. Reproduced by permission.

In 1998 the Linguistic Society of America also affirmed this basic human right. It passed a resolution supporting the right of all residents of the United States "to have their children educated in a manner that affirmatively acknowledges their native language abilities as well as ensures their acquisition of English."

Not only is the right to learn in one's native language a human right, it is a civil right as well. In 1974, the U.S. Supreme Court ruled in *Lau vs. Nichols* that California schools without special provisions to educate language minority students were violating the students' civil rights. This decision gave impetus to the bilingual education movement.

Policies That Harm Children

In our minds, the civil right to an equal opportunity in education is clearly violated when children are denied an education that is comprehensible. If students are placed in "English immersion" classes large chunks of the curriculum will be incomprehensible. This violates a basic civil right to equal treatment under the law.

We are disturbed by the way voters are manipulated by money and disinformation to vote for policies that harm children, but it's difficult to hold individual voters accountable for their actions. However, elected officials who voted for the ESEA can and should be held accountable for their actions.

Any hope of overturning the current anti-bilingual policies begins with students, families, and educators. We need to show state and federal legislators how their discriminatory policies affect children and force them to change their positions before the ESEA comes up for reauthorization. . . .

As educators who believe in social justice we think it is important to fight for everyone's human and civil rights. Ultimately, we believe that all children should have the right to learn at least two languages, including their mother tongue. Throughout the world children become bilingual or multilingual and it is valued. We call upon everyone who believes in bilingual education to testify, organize, and demand that our childrens' rights be restored and protected.

*"If this trend [toward bilingualism]
continues, the cultural division between
Hispanics and Anglos could replace the
racial division between blacks and whites."*

Bilingual Education Threatens the Cultural Unity of America

Samuel Huntington

In the following viewpoint Samuel Huntington asserts that bilingual education threatens the cultural unity of the United States. Immigrants from Mexico and other Spanish-speaking countries are increasingly less likely to learn English, he maintains, and bilingual education only exacerbates the problem. Native English speakers are put at a political and economic disadvantage, Huntington argues, as the acceptance of Spanish grows in the United States. Bilingual education thus fosters a language divide in America, he claims. Huntington is chairman of the Harvard Academy for International and Area Studies.

As you read, consider the following questions:

1. According to Huntington, how do second- and third-generation Mexican Americans differ from other second- and third-generation immigrants?
2. In Miami, what is the average income for families speaking only Spanish? Only English? For bilingual families?
3. What sentiment regarding bilingualism did Bill Clinton express in a June 2000 speech?

Samuel Huntington, "The Hispanic Challenge," *Foreign Policy*, March/April 2004. Copyright © 2004 by Samuel P. Huntington. Reproduced by permission.

In the past, immigrants originated overseas and often over-
came severe obstacles and hardships to reach the United
States. They came from many different countries, spoke different languages, and came legally. Their flow fluctuated
over time, with significant reductions occurring as a result of
the Civil War, World War I, and the restrictive legislation of
1924. They dispersed into many enclaves in rural areas and
major cities throughout the Northeast and Midwest. They
had no historical claim to any U.S. territory.

On all these dimensions, Mexican immigration is fundamentally different. These differences combine to make the
assimilation of Mexicans into U.S. culture and society much
more difficult than it was for previous immigrants. Particularly striking in contrast to previous immigrants is the failure of third- and fourth-generation people of Mexican origin to approximate U.S. norms in education, economic
status, and intermarriage rates.

The size, persistence, and concentration of Hispanic immigration tends to perpetuate the use of Spanish through
successive generations. The evidence on English acquisition
and Spanish retention among immigrants is limited and ambiguous. In 2000, however, more than 28 million people in
the United States spoke Spanish at home (10.5 percent of all
people over age five), and almost 13.8 million of these spoke
English worse than "very well," a 66 percent increase since
1990. According to a U.S. Census Bureau report, in 1990
about 95 percent of Mexican-born immigrants spoke Spanish at home; 73.6 percent of these did not speak English very
well; and 43 percent of the Mexican foreign-born were "linguistically isolated." An earlier study in Los Angeles found
different results for the U.S.-born second generation. Just
11.6 percent spoke only Spanish or more Spanish than English, 25.6 percent spoke both languages equally, 32.7 percent more English than Spanish, and 30.1 percent only English. In the same study, more than 90 percent of the
U.S.-born people of Mexican origin spoke English fluently.
Nonetheless, in 1999, some 753,505 presumably second-
generation students in Southern California schools who
spoke Spanish at home were not proficient in English.

English language use and fluency for first- and second-generation Mexicans thus seem to follow the pattern common to past immigrants. Two questions remain, however. First, have changes occurred over time in the acquisition of English and the retention of Spanish by second-generation Mexican immigrants? One might suppose that, with the rapid expansion of the Mexican immigrant community, people of Mexican origin would have less incentive to become fluent in and to use English in 2000 than they had in 1970.

Second, will the third generation follow the classic pattern with fluency in English and little or no knowledge of Spanish, or will it retain the second generation's fluency in both languages? Second-generation immigrants often look down on and reject their ancestral language and are embarrassed by their parents' inability to communicate in English. Presumably, whether second-generation Mexicans share this attitude will help shape the extent to which the third generation retains any knowledge of Spanish. If the second generation does not reject Spanish outright, the third generation is also likely to be bilingual, and fluency in both languages is likely to become institutionalized in the Mexican-American community.

Spanish retention is also bolstered by the overwhelming majorities (between 66 percent and 85 percent) of Mexican immigrants and Hispanics who emphasize the need for their children to be fluent in Spanish. These attitudes contrast with those of other immigrant groups. The New Jersey-based Educational Testing Service finds "a cultural difference between the Asian and Hispanic parents with respect to having their children maintain their native language." In part, this difference undoubtedly stems from the size of Hispanic communities, which creates incentives for fluency in the ancestral language. Although second- and third-generation Mexican Americans and other Hispanics acquire competence in English, they also appear to deviate from the usual pattern by maintaining their competence in Spanish. Second- or third-generation Mexican Americans who were brought up speaking only English have learned Spanish as adults and are encouraging their children to become fluent in it. Spanish-language competence, University of New Mexico professor F. Chris Garcia has stated, is "the one thing every Hispanic takes pride in, wants to protect and promote."

Two Languages or One?

A persuasive case can be made that, in a shrinking world, all Americans should know at least one important foreign language—Chinese, Japanese, Hindi, Russian, Arabic, Urdu, French, German, or Spanish—so as to understand a foreign culture and communicate with its people. It is quite different to argue that Americans should know a non-English language in order to communicate with their fellow citizens. Yet that is what the Spanish-language advocates have in mind. Strengthened by the growth of Hispanic numbers and influence, Hispanic leaders are actively seeking to transform the United States into a bilingual society. "English is not enough," argues Osvaldo Soto, president of the Spanish American League Against Discrimination. "We don't want a monolingual society." Similarly, Duke University literature professor (and Chilean immigrant) Ariel Dorfman asks, "Will this country speak two languages or merely one?" And his answer, of course, is that it should speak two.

Hispanic organizations play a central role in inducing the U.S. Congress to authorize cultural maintenance programs in bilingual education; as a result, children are slow to join mainstream classes. The continuing huge inflow of migrants makes it increasingly possible for Spanish speakers in New York, Miami, and Los Angeles to live normal lives without knowing English. Sixty-five percent of the children in bilingual education in New York are Spanish speakers and hence have little incentive or need to use English in school.

Dual-language programs, which go one step beyond bilingual education, have become increasingly popular. In these programs, students are taught in both English and Spanish on an alternating basis with a view to making English-speakers fluent in Spanish and Spanish-speakers fluent in English, thus making Spanish the equal of English and transforming the United States into a two-language country. Then U.S. Secretary of Education Richard Riley explicitly endorsed these programs in his March 2000 speech, "Excelencia para Todos—Excellence for all." Civil rights organizations, church leaders (particularly Catholic ones), and many politicians (Republican as well as Democrat) support the impetus toward bilingualism.

The Number of Non-English Speakers Is on the Rise

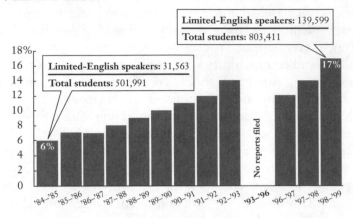

Limited-English speakers: 139,599
Total students: 803,411

Limited-English speakers: 31,563
Total students: 501,991

6%

17%

No reports filed

'84–'85 '85–'86 '86–'87 '87–'88 '88–'89 '89–'90 '90–'91 '91–'92 '92–'93 '93–'96 '96–'97 '97–'98 '98–'99

Arizona Department of Education, cited in *Arizona Daily Star*, April 11, 2000.

Perhaps equally important, business groups seeking to corner the Hispanic market support bilingualism as well. Indeed, the orientation of U.S. businesses to Hispanic customers means they increasingly need bilingual employees; therefore, bilingualism is affecting earnings. Bilingual police officers and firefighters in southwestern cities such as Phoenix and Las Vegas are paid more than those who only speak English. In Miami, one study found, families that spoke only Spanish had average incomes of $18,000; English-only families had average incomes of $32,000; and bilingual families averaged more than $50,000. For the first time in U.S. history, increasing numbers of Americans (particularly black Americans) will not be able to receive the jobs or the pay they would otherwise receive because they can speak to their fellow citizens only in English.

One Flag, One Language?

In the debates over language policy, the late California Republican Senator S.I. Hayakawa once highlighted the unique role of Hispanics in opposing English. "Why is it that no Filipinos, no Koreans object to making English the official language? No Japanese have done so. And certainly not the Vietnamese, who are so damn happy to be here. They're learning English as fast as they can and winning spelling bees all across

94

the country. But the Hispanics alone have maintained there is a problem. There [has been] considerable movement to make Spanish the second official language."

If the spread of Spanish as the United States' second language continues, it could, in due course, have significant consequences in politics and government. In many states, those aspiring to political office might have to be fluent in both languages. Bilingual candidates for president and elected federal positions would have an advantage over English-only speakers. If dual-language education becomes prevalent in elementary and secondary schools, teachers will increasingly be expected to be bilingual. Government documents and forms could routinely be published in both languages. The use of both languages could become acceptable in congressional hearings and debates and in the general conduct of government business. Because most of those whose first language is Spanish will also probably have some fluency in English, English speakers lacking fluency in Spanish are likely to be and feel at a disadvantage in the competition for jobs, promotions, and contracts.

In 1917, former U.S. President Theodore Roosevelt said: "We must have but one flag. We must also have but one language. That must be the language of the Declaration of Independence, of Washington's Farewell address, of Lincoln's Gettysburg speech and second inaugural." By contrast, in June 2000, U.S. president Bill Clinton said, "I hope very much that I'm the last president in American history who can't speak Spanish." And in May 2001, President Bush celebrated Mexico's Cinco de Mayo national holiday by inaugurating the practice of broadcasting the weekly presidential radio address to the American people in both English and Spanish. In September 2003, one of the first debates among the Democratic Party's presidential candidates also took place in both English and Spanish. Despite the opposition of large majorities of Americans, Spanish is joining the language of Washington, Jefferson, Lincoln, the Roosevelts, and the Kennedys as the language of the United States. If this trend continues, the cultural division between Hispanics and Anglos could replace the racial division between blacks and whites as the most serious cleavage in U.S. society.

"Americans today, even after an attack on our nation, are more welcoming than ever."

The War on Terrorism Improves Immigrant Relations

Michael Barone

In the following viewpoint Michael Barone contends that since the terrorist attacks of September 11, 2001, Americans welcome immigrants more than ever. The war on terrorism, Barone claims, elicited support from new and native-born Americans alike. In fact, he maintains, in the months following the attacks, applications for U.S. citizenship soared. Acts of reprisal against Muslim and Arab Americans have been rare and are overshadowed by acts of support, Barone asserts. Barone, a senior writer for *U.S. News & World Report*, is also the author of *The New Americans: How the Melting Pot Can Work Again*.

As you read, consider the following questions:

1. What evidence does Barone cite for his claim that support for the war on terrorism cuts across racial groups?
2. What percentage of people serving in the Marine Corps does the author claim are Hispanic?
3. What does Barone contend is lacking in most Muslim Arab nations?

The response of today's immigrants to the [terrorist attacks] of September 11, 2001, was very much like the response of earlier immigrants to Pearl Harbor. In fact, it was very much like the response of all Americans to September 11: We have been attacked, and we will respond. It was lost on no one that the victims at the World Trade Center and the Pentagon included immigrants, both new citizens and foreign nationals, in large numbers.

All Americans Support the War on Terror

And who can forget the scene when George W. Bush came to Ground Zero on Friday, September 14? Someone yelled that he couldn't hear him. Bush responded, unscripted, "I can hear you. The whole world can hear you. And the people who knocked down these buildings will hear from all of us soon." Immediately the crowd of rescue workers began chanting, "U.S.A.! U.S.A.! U.S.A.!" As the camera panned in on them, the viewer could see that under the yellow hats were faces of all kinds of Americans, of all complexions and races and ethnic origins. And their message was: We are all Americans.

Ever since, it has been plain that support for the war against terrorism among new Americans is as high as it is among Americans generally. Poll results show no difference between Latinos or Asians and other Americans on war-related issues. American flags were seen in the same profusion in Latino neighborhoods as in the rural Midwest and South (indeed, rapidly growing numbers of Latinos live in the rural Midwest and South). Cab drivers from Pakistan and Ethiopia proudly displayed American flags. Applications for citizenship soared in the months following 9/11: over 60 percent more immigrants applied in that period than in the same period the year before. In south Florida, immigrants from many Latin American countries watching the World Cup games referred to the U.S. team as the team of *todos los nosotros*—the team of all of us. America is our country, they seem to be saying, loudly and proudly, and as strongly as any American whose ancestors have been here for many generations.

The war against terrorism does not present as many opportunities for military service as did World War II; we no longer have a draft, and the size of U.S. armed forces does not seem likely to be substantially increased. But Latinos already serve in large numbers in the military: in September 2001, there were over a hundred thousand Hispanic enlisted men and women, representing about 9.5 percent of active-duty military personnel. Their participation is especially great in the Marine Corps, where nearly 14 percent of enlisted personnel are Hispanic—possibly because the Marines have resisted the feminist-inspired move toward a less macho culture that has affected the other services. (Citizenship is not required for military service, and many noncitizen Latinos served in Iraq. Two were killed and were posthumously granted U.S. citizenship; George W. Bush stood by in a room at Bethesda Naval Hospital as a wounded serviceman was sworn in as a U.S. citizen.) Asians already work in large numbers in the high-tech industries that are so important to the creation of the precision-guided weapons and sophisticated electronic communications systems used by our high-tech military force.

The Reaction of Muslim Arabs

The one identifiable group that seems not to have joined wholeheartedly in the war against terrorism is Muslim Arabs. Official Islamic organizations have made only perfunctory denunciations of the September 11 attacks, and have given only perfunctory support to the war against terrorism. Their spokesmen have been much more vociferous in opposing measures taken in the war effort and in asserting claims that civil liberties have been violated (though civil liberties are for the most part nonexistent in every Muslim Arab nation).

These actions are evidently prompted by fear of a xenophobic reaction against Muslims and Arabs. But there have been only a few such acts of violence in a nation of 285 million people. Much more frequent have been spontaneous acts of friendliness and reassurance directed at people of Muslim and Arab origin by Americans of all descriptions. Public officials, starting with then Mayor Rudolph Giuliani and President George W. Bush, have spoken out vigorously and often against any negative reaction to Muslims and Arabs generally. Bush has often said that America is fighting not Islam but terrorism. Indeed, public officials have been reluctant to label even obvious acts of terrorism as such—notably the July 4, 2002 attack by an Egyptian on the El Al counter in Los Angeles International Airport. This is a country bending over backwards not to engage in acts like the persecution of German-Americans in World War I and the internment of Japanese-Americans in World War II.

Unique Among Nations

In the early twentieth century, the United States was unique among nations in its response to immigrants and new citizens: we were more welcoming to newcomers, and we insisted more strongly on assimilation. The United States that was attacked on September 11 had changed somewhat. We are now, if anything, still more welcoming to newcomers than we were a century ago. Overt bigotry has greatly diminished, even as the heritage of the immigrant experience in this country is still vividly recalled. But at the same time, we are less insistent on assimilation than we used to be; today, the word "Americanization" sounds harsh and even bigoted to many ears.

New York's Greatest Strength

When the terrorists attacked the World Trade Center hundreds of immigrants perished with native Americans. New York misses them sorely, along with its natives who were also killed, as members of its own family. Fortunately, New York continues to make its immigrants feel welcome. . . . This is New York's greatest strength despite being the victim of the worst terrorist attack in history. New York City, which suffered the most devastation on that fateful morning of September 11, is still an example to the rest of the country for continuing to lay out the welcoming mat toward immigrants.

Cyrus D. Mehta, "Immigrants Are Ever More Crucial After 9/11," *Immigration Daily*, September 25, 2002. www.ilw.com.

My prediction is that September 11 and the response to it will change this trend. America will still welcome immigrants, despite fears that our borders may be vulnerable to terrorists. But we will no longer embrace the notion that it is somehow oppressive to encourage assimilation and Americanization.

America's welcoming attitude towards immigrants will not change because it is deeply rooted in the hearts and histories of the American people. John F. Kennedy, the first president of post-1840 immigrant stock, memorably said that the United States is "a nation of immigrants." And in fact most Americans today—thanks to the volume of immigration and to the intermarriage of people who were once thought to be of different "races"—are descended at least partly from immigrants who came here after 1840. If it is a tendency of Europeans to identify with the most ennobled of their forebears, it is the habit of Americans to identify with the humblest.

This habit was strengthened by the ceremonies commemorating the one hundredth anniversary of the Statue of Liberty in 1986; it is witnessed by the popularity of the Ellis Island website; it is evident in the happy profusion of ethnic cuisines of immigrants new and old. Americans are inclined to tell pollsters that immigration should be reduced somewhat from current levels. But there is no political strength behind the idea, advanced by Patrick Buchanan and others, to cut off immigration altogether. Nor has there been great political strength behind proposals to reduce immigration sharply for fear of terrorist infiltration. Americans looking at immigrants today realize that their own ancestors once lived in similar situations.

More Welcoming than Ever

This helps to explain the benign response of the great mass of Americans to Arabs and Muslims in their midst. Some unknown number of Muslims living in this country cheered the September 11 attacks, and believe that in a battle, as they see it, between Islam and the United States, they will support Islam. But this fact is largely ignored; most non-Muslim Americans assume hopefully that such people are few in number. There seems to be no great appetite for cracking down on the Saudi-financed Wahhabi-run mosques and *madrassas* and Islamic organizations that, in the United States as well as other places, preach terror and hatred of Americans and Jews. The government's refusal to single out young Arab or Muslim males for special scrutiny at airport checkpoints elicits little loud opposition. It is more important, evidently, to avoid "racial profiling" and ethnic discrimination. Proposals to change immigration law have gotten no serious hearing. Americans today, even after an attack on our nation, are more welcoming than ever. . . .

September 11 gave great strength to the idea that, for all our cultural differences, we are one nation, united in support of great principles, ready to work together to preserve the decent society in which we live. It has undermined the assumption of the elites, a hangover from the 1960s, that America is an indecent or unworthy society, its people so vicious that they must be tamed by the constant social engineering of an enlightened elite to keep them from oppressing others. The new Americans' solid support for the American war against terrorism show that they share the majority's vision of America as a decent society. And their contributions to the war effort show that they are doing their share to make sure our common values prevail.

The war against terrorism will prove to be a unifying event for new Americans, just as wars have been for earlier generations of immigrants. But, perhaps as important, it also seems likely to be a unifying event for the American elites, who for four decades have doubted the decency of their country and tried to retard the process of assimilation. Americanization has worked in the past, and it will work once again to weave new Americans into the national fabric—one that will be stronger and richer and more vivid for their presence.

"Within two weeks after the [terrorist attacks of September 11, 2001,] my youngest daughter, Tennessee, was called a dirty Arab, twice."

The War on Terrorism Harms Immigrant Relations

Ishmael Reed

In the following viewpoint Ishmael Reed argues that in the wake of the September 11, 2001, terrorist attacks, immigrants and minorities, particularly Arab Americans, face increasing discrimination. Antiterrorist laws have led to the arrest and detention of thousands of Arab American immigrants. People who simply have dark skin have been unfairly identified as terrorists, he claims. In fact, Reed asserts, it was most likely because his skin is dark that he was singled out by airport security at the San Francisco airport. Reed, a poet, novelist, and songwriter, teaches at the University of California, Berkeley.

As you read, consider the following questions:
1. What irony does Reed find in the current targeting of Arab Americans?
2. What countries (in addition to the United States) use military tribunals?
3. According to the author, how did groups persecuted during World War II "become white"?

Ishmael Reed, *Another Day at the Front.* New York: Basic Books, 2003. Copyright © 2003 by Basic Books. Reproduced by permission of Basic Books, a member of Perseus Books, L.L.C and in the UK by Lowenstein-Yost Associates, Inc.

M y mother named me after her favorite cousin, and a few weeks ago at the St. Louis airport, the salesperson asked me whether I was a Muslim. I said no, but when I arrived at the baggage claims section at the San Francisco airport, I noticed that mine was the only luggage with a red tag attached to it. Maybe the red tag meant "this is a wonderful person," but how would I know? It was an unsettling experience.

Targeting an Entire Community

Within two weeks after the WTC [World Trade Center] and Pentagon bombings [on September 11, 2001], my youngest daughter, Tennessee, was called a dirty Arab, twice. An elderly white woman made such a scene on a San Francisco bus that my daughter got off. That time, she was wearing a scarf that I bought her in Egypt . . . but on the other occasion there was nothing distinctive about her clothing. Some of the post–9-11 profiling would be comic and ironic if the circumstances weren't so tragic. Marvin X, an African-American playwright, has been criticizing some Arab-American owners of ghetto stores for selling pork, alcohol, and drugs and extending credit to poor women in exchange for sexual favors. A few days after the terrorist attack, he was surrounded by men with guns at Newark airport. They mistook him for an Arab terrorist.

The experience of me, my daughter, and Marvin X points to the problem with flashing a searchlight upon an entire community, which is what's being done to Arab-Americans by many white Americans, who've become apprehensive as they move about their daily lives.

But who's Arab? A few years ago, journalist Earl Caldwell and I entertained over thirty Arab journalists at the Maynard Institute in Oakland. Their escort, an Arab-American attorney, said that he'd been stopped, while driving an expensive car, because the police mistook him for a black American. Is anyone with a dark skin Arab-American? Should those who are caught in the net meant for Arab-Americans follow the example of some Chinese-Americans who, when the Japanese-Americans were herded into detention camps, wore signs that read "I Am Chinese"?

The Bush administration has taken advantage of the hysteria that's been ignited by the media and other institutions to jam a "Patriot" bill through Congress.[1] This bill gives the executive branch tremendous powers with very little judicial review. The government detained over a thousand people, some of them incommunicado, and refused to identify who is being detained and why when requested to do so by Senator Russ Feingold. The administration wants to monitor communications between lawyers and their clients. The Justice Department is questioning 5,000 Muslim men, a procedure that Feingold describes as "offensive" and "intrusive." They established military tribunals without consulting the Defense Department or Congress. (Military tribunals that are opposed by the Spanish government!)

A Threat to Native-Born and Immigrant Americans

The USA PATRIOT Act:

Creates a broad definition of "domestic terrorism" that may have a chilling effect on the US and international rights to free expression and association. The law defines "domestic terrorism" as acts committed in the United States "dangerous to human life that are a violation of the criminal laws," if the US government determines that they "appear to be intended" to "influence the policy of a government by intimidation or coercion," or "to intimidate or coerce a civilian population." Such ambiguous language allows for loose interpretation that might violate civil liberties and international human rights.

Allows non-citizens to be detained without charge and held indefinitely once charged. This is permissible if the US government certifies that there are "reasonable grounds" to believe a person's action threatens national security. This runs counter to US and international rights to due process and could also lead to violations of rights in the Vienna Convention on Consular Relations, which guarantee that governments be notified if their nationals are detained.

Amnesty International, "'War on Terror' Human Rights Issues," Amnesty International Web site, 2005. www.amnestyusa.org.

Given President Bush's switch-happy record as Texas executioner, I'd hate to be one of those tried. Senator Edward Kennedy has criticized such tribunals for their lack of "open-

1. The USA PATRIOT Act was signed into law October 26, 2001.

ness" and "fairness" and "due process." Burma, Nigeria, Turkey, and Egypt are among the countries where such military tribunals are used. Now the United States.

Some have complained that the United States is becoming a "banana republic" as a result of the 9-11 events. William Safire, a *New York Times* columnist and a genuine conservative (not just one who plays the role on TV), calls these powers "dictatorial."

Arab-Americans won't be the first group to be singled out for scorn as a result of international events over which they have no control. Professor Lois Fassbinder writes about the prejudice her German-American family experienced during World War II. During the same war, hundreds of Italian immigrants were interned and thousands had their travel restricted by the Justice Department. Italian-Americans were forced from their homes and required to submit to hearings before military tribunals. Some members of both groups were able to deal with such humiliation by turning "white" —an option that is open to those with white skins and maybe open to white-skinned Arab-Americans. (As Malcolm X discovered during his trip to the Middle East, Islam includes members of all races.) They can change their names and disappear into the white world.

The Drawbacks of Assimilation

But this has its drawbacks, too. A few years ago, I was a panelist at an Irish-American writers conference. At the end of the panel, I asked members of the audience if assimilation had been worth it. None of the audience members said yes. Some complained that they had to change their names and marry Anglos in order to get jobs. They had to give up their roots.

Decades after World War II, the United States apologized to the Japanese-American community for the internment but, judging from the complaints of some contemporary Japanese-American poets and novelists who were children in those camps, the psychic scars remain.

With the exception of Native Americans, however, no group has been terrorized as much as African-Americans by the kind of homegrown terrorists about whom the Justice Department seems indifferent. Maybe the experience of

African-Americans will be a guide to all Americans about how to handle both profiling and terrorism.

Martin Luther King Jr. was an object of hate crimes and his home was bombed. He didn't go into a funk and yield to his tormentors, but persisted. Both Booker T. Washington and Frederick Douglass were born slaves; their lives were at risk every day. In their lectures, they always warned their white audiences that if such outrages could happen to blacks they could happen to them as well. Now the president and the attorney general are hunting Arab-Americans. Who's next?

Periodical Bibliography

The following articles have been selected to supplement the diverse views presented in this chapter.

Jim Boulet Jr.   "Assimilation, Not Amnesty," *National Review*, August 21, 2001.

Jorge Capetillo-Ponce   "Challenges to Multiculturalism," University of Massachusetts Boston. www.mccormack.umb.edu/nejpp/articles/20_1/ChallengestoMulticulturalism.pdf

Roberto Clemente   "Language: Cultural Identity and Bilingualism of Latino/as in an Anglo-American Context," *Hispanic Outlook in Higher Education*, October 9, 2000.

Economist   "Welcome, Stranger," September 6, 2001.

Federation for American Immigration Reform   "Chicano Nationalism, Revanchism, and the Aztlan Myth," Fairus.org, January 2005. www.fairus.org/site/PageServer?pagename=iic_immigrationissuecenters861a.

J.A. Foster-Bey   "Not Black and White," *National Review*, September 27, 2004.

John Greenya   "Immigration Law in Post–9-11 America," *DC Bar*, August 2003.

Tamar Jacoby   "How to Turn More Immigrants into Americans," *New York Sun*, July 3, 2002.

Mark Krikorian   "Taking Two Steps Back for Every Step Forward on Immigration," *National Review*, August 14, 2004.

Jose R. Martinez   "Unspoken Fear Among Hispanics," *Denver Post*, November 3, 2004.

Clarence Page   "At Colleges, Immigrants Are 'Minorities' Too," *Chicago Tribune*, July 7, 2004.

Sam Roberts   "More Africans Enter U.S. than in Days of Slavery," *New York Times*, February 21, 2005.

Simon Romero and Janet Elder   "Hispanics in the U.S. Report Optimism," *New York Times*, August 6, 2003.

Hector A. Torres   "I Don't Think I Exist: Interview with Richard Rodriguez," *MELUS*, Summer 2003.

CHAPTER 3

What Policies Promote Opportunities for All Races?

Chapter Preface

The idea of busing for the purpose of integrating schools was legally sanctioned in the 1971 U.S. Supreme Court case *Swann v. Charlotte-Mecklenberg Board of Education.* In this case the Court approved busing as a way to remedy residential segregation in schools. In the late 1990s many school districts eliminated busing. As a result, previously integrated schools have again become segregated. Proponents argue that busing allows minority children to attend better schools, and the resulting integration helps eliminate racial prejudice. Opponents contend that busing is not good for education and isolates minority children from their community.

Busing opponents claim that desegregation has been detrimental to the American educational system. According to activists Marc Levin and Ed Blum, "What began as an effort to remedy the grave wrongs of state-sanctioned racial segregation has turned American society—black and white—on its head. The neighborhood school concept, with the pride and solidarity it engenders in a community, has been badly damaged for the last three decades [by busing]." Not only are children denied the educational advantages of going to school within the same community where they live, opponents argue, they are also forced to endure long hours on the school bus, which cuts into time spent with family or studying. The practice also tacitly endorses racial discrimination, Levin and Blum assert. "Rather than eliminating racial discrimination," they maintain, "busing promotes it by teaching children that the government should treat them differently on the basis of their race."

Supporters of busing, on the other hand, have expressed concern that dismantling busing will bring about a return to unequal access to education and contend that minority children will end up suffering as a result. Because minority neighborhoods often do not have the economic resources that white neighborhoods have, an end to busing often means, for minority students, an end to greater opportunity. "The white kids get neighborhood schools, the minority kids get inferior schools," says Gary Orfield, an education and social policy professor at Harvard University and director of the Harvard

Project on School Desegregation. Proponents of busing assert that minority students are not the only students who benefit from integration. The Common Sense Foundation, a nonpartisan public policy organization, claims that "the interaction between racial groups in integrated settings can dramatically change what people think of and how they act toward people of other races. Integration is the first step toward eliminating racial stereotypes and prejudice."

Advocates on both sides of this issue want what is best for America's children. Identifying which policies are best for people of all races is rarely clear-cut, as the viewpoints in the following chapter demonstrate.

"Affirmative action is essential to guarantee people of color, minorities, and women equality in employment and education."

Affirmative Action Allows Minorities to Compete Fairly

Hector M. Flores

In the following viewpoint, taken from a speech delivered on May 29, 2003, Hector M. Flores argues that affirmative action is necessary to counter deeply entrenched racism and practices that favor whites. According to Flores, minorities are underrepresented in various fields. Although studies show the positive effects of affirmative action, it is only effective when enforced, which, Flores maintains, is not always the case. Stringently enforced affirmative action is still necessary to allow minorities to compete on an equal footing with whites, Flores contends. Flores is national president of the League of United Latin American Citizens.

As you read, consider the following questions:

1. What sort of buzzwords does Flores accuse politicians of using to tar affirmative action programs?
2. According to data provided by the author, what percent of lawyers are white men? What percent are black? Latino?
3. According to the Joint Center for Political and Economic Studies, why have the benefits of affirmative action been quite small?

Hector M. Flores, "Affirmative Action," Leadership Conference on Civil Rights, www.civilrights.org, May 29, 2003. Reproduced by permission.

It is indeed a pleasure to be here with you to address affirmative action, an issue of great importance to me and the organization over which I preside.

I would like to preface my remarks by briefly telling about the League of United Latin American Citizens better known as LULAC.

As the national president of LULAC, I am well aware of the historic battles waged by minorities and women for equal opportunity in this country. In its 66 year history, LULAC has been on the front lines of the Hispanic community's struggle against discrimination.

LULAC strongly supports equal opportunity for employment, promotion and contracting, as well as equal access to quality educational opportunities that will empower our youth for success. LULAC firmly believes that affirmative action is essential to guarantee people of color, minorities, and women equality in employment and education.

Taking Positive Steps

Otherwise, the racism and discrimination that continues to surface through many forms—proposition 187 in California, anti-immigrant bashing, "English only" sentiments, etc.— will become the norm in academia and the work environment. We and the proponents of affirmative action do not want handouts in employment, education, and public contracts. What we want is really quite simple: the right to compete and participate on a level playing field, equal access and equal opportunity. We see affirmative action as a set of positive steps that employers, educators, administrators, and governmental agencies use to promote and achieve equal employment opportunities.

I truly believe that the "Good-Old-Boys Network"[1] is alive and well and that in today's work place, deeply, entrenched, racial and gender bias against minorities and women still exists. Affirmative action is necessary to help level the playing field. Those who oppose affirmative action, directly or indirectly, are inviting wholesale racial and gen-

---

1. An informal, exclusive system of mutual assistance and friendship, in which favors are exchanged. A "good old boy" is a man who has characteristics of a southern white male: often intolerant and anti-intellectual.

der discrimination into the work place.

President [Bill] Clinton called for a comprehensive review of the Federal Affirmative Action programs and LULAC fully supports the President. In particular, LULAC favors strengthening these programs so that they will better address the needs of the Hispanic community.

The political rhetoric against affirmative action by several presidential candidates and key Members of Congress needs to be taken very seriously. This issue is particularly sensitive at a time of corporate downsizing and major reductions in federal employment. Those fighting to defeat affirmative action are winning the war of perception in the media, newspapers, and with ordinary citizens. Their success has been largely due to the utilization of such buzzwords, such as "quotas", "preferential treatment", and "lowering standards" that have helped them define the affirmative action debate, playing on the fears of the uninformed.

Casting a Wider Net

We have been slow in defining affirmative action and have failed to get the public response generated by the opposition. Affirmative action merely casts a wider net to include a larger number of qualified applicants to compete and participate. Affirmative action allows women and people of color and other minorities access to higher education, jobs, and business opportunities which have been historically out of their reach. Affirmative action is a system of goals and programs that strengthens our national economy. It provides Corporate America with the diversity necessary to compete in the global market. It helps to ensure that the public sector is reflective of the populations it serves. Quotas and preferential treatment have never been a part of any affirmative action program.

[Former U.S. senator] Bob Dole says that equal opportunity without affirmative action should be the nation's goal. What a great concept! However, as much as we would like, we don't live in a colorblind society. Discrimination is alive and well in this country.

In spite of the opportunities afforded minorities and women, we are still not the ones benefiting in the work

Thompson. © by Copley News Service. Reproduced by permission.

place, on university campuses, and from public contracts-white males are. On a national level, women represent 51.2% of the adult population, African Americans represent 12.4%, and Latinos represent 9.5%. Yet in the labor market:

- 69% of all doctors are white men, 22% are white women, 4% are Black, and only 5% are Latino.
- 70% of all lawyers are white men, 24% are white women, 3% are Black, and 3% are Latino.
- 80% of all architects are white men, 16% are white women, 1% are Black, and 1% are Latino.
- 85% of all engineers are white men, 8% are white women, 4% are Black, and 3% are Latino.
- In Texas alone, 81% of all CEOs, executives, and business managers are white, 11% are Latino, 6% are Black, while Asians and other minorities make up only 2%.

A Long Way to Go

These findings are echoed in a report from the Joint Center for Political and Economic Studies in Washington. The report shows that affirmative action programs have had "some positive effects in opening new opportunities for minorities, but that the measurable benefits in terms of wages and employment have been quite small." The report concludes, "While affirmative action can be an effective policy tool, its impact is related to the vigor with which it's enforced." In addition, the Bureau of Labor Statistics figures show that in 1994 whites held 88.8% of managerial and professional positions, down only slightly from 91.6% in 1983.

So where is the reverse discrimination all the "angry white men" are talking about? In a recent study published [in March 2003], the U.S. Department of Labor examined opinions handed down by U. S. District Courts and Courts of Appeals regarding employment discrimination cases between 1990 and 1994. Of the 3,000 employment discrimination opinions, fewer than 100 were reverse discrimination claims, and, of those, only 12 were found to have any merit. Professor Alfred Blumrosen, author of the analysis and a law professor at Rutgers University, wrote "many of the Cases were the result of a disappointed applicant failing to examine his or her own qualifications."

Jim Rogers of WBAP [a radio station] in Dallas/Fort Worth describes "the typical angry white guy" as being "fearful of the evolving global economy, concerned about affirmative action programs seen as 'reverse discrimination,' and resentful of Washington and the Federal government, for what they perceive as loss of freedom, loss of income, loss of opportunity and loss of confidence."

All of which is just a perception. The facts clearly state that women and people of color still have a long way to go to reach equality in the work place—affirmative action is not a threat to anyone.

Affirmative Action is not only the right thing to do but it is also good for our Country. We must not hesitate to take a stand and commit to educate our communities to gain their support on this important issue. Just as our forefathers fought to achieve civil rights so must we fight to retain those rights.

"These [affirmative action] programs stamp minorities with a badge of inferiority and may cause them to develop dependencies."

Affirmative Action Hinders Minorities

Clarence Thomas

In 2003 the U.S. Supreme Court decided to strike down the University of Michigan's undergraduate admissions affirmative action program in *Gratz v. Bollinger* while upholding the graduate admissions program in *Grutter v. Bollinger*. In the following viewpoint, excerpted from his dissenting opinion in *Grutter*, U.S. Supreme Court justice Clarence Thomas argues that affirmative action hurts minorities. Affirmative action policies do not push minority students to achieve, asserts Thomas. Therefore, minority students do not score as highly on standardized tests, maintaining the myth of their inferiority.

As you read, consider the following questions:
1. According to Thomas, why does the U.S. Constitution prohibit classifications based on race?
2. What lies beneath the Court's majority opinion in *Grutter v. Bollinger*, in the author's view?
3. In the author's opinion, why are all blacks admitted to law school tarred as undeserving?

Clarence Thomas, opinion, *Barbara Grutter, Petitioner v. Lee Bollinger et al.*, U.S. Supreme Court, June 23, 2003.

[E]arly civil rights activist] Frederick Douglass, speaking to a group of abolitionists almost 140 years ago, delivered a message lost on today's majority:

> In regard to the colored people, there is always more that is benevolent, I perceive, than just, manifested towards us. What I ask for the negro is not benevolence, not pity, not sympathy, but simply *justice*. The American people have always been anxious to know what they shall do with us. . . . I have had but one answer from the beginning. Do nothing with us! Your doing with us has already played the mischief with us. Do nothing with us! If the apples will not remain on the tree of their own strength, if they are worm-eaten at the core, if they are early ripe and disposed to fall, let them fall! . . . And if the negro cannot stand on his own legs, let him fall also. All I ask is, give him a chance to stand on his own legs! Let him alone! . . . Your interference is doing him positive injury. "What the Black Man Wants: An Address Delivered in Boston, Massachusetts, on 26 January 1865.". . .

Like Douglass, I believe blacks can achieve in every avenue of American life without the meddling of university administrators. Because I wish to see all students succeed whatever their color, I share, in some respect, the sympathies of those who sponsor the type of discrimination advanced by the University of Michigan Law School (Law School) [under its affirmative action admissions policies]. The Constitution does not, however, tolerate institutional devotion to the status quo in admissions policies when such devotion ripens into racial discrimination. Nor does the Constitution countenance the unprecedented deference the Court gives to the Law School, an approach inconsistent with the very concept of "strict scrutiny."

An Exclusionary Policy

No one would argue that a university could set up a lower general admission standard and then impose heightened requirements only on black applicants. Similarly, a university may not maintain a high admission standard and grant exemptions to favored races. The Law School, of its own choosing, and for its own purposes, maintains an exclusionary admissions system that it knows produces racially disproportionate results. Racial discrimination is not a permissible solution to

117

the self-inflicted wounds of this elitist admissions policy.

The majority upholds the Law School's racial discrimination not by interpreting the people's Constitution, but by responding to a faddish slogan of the cognoscenti. Nevertheless, I concur in part in the Court's opinion. First, I agree with the Court insofar as its decision, which approves of only one racial classification, confirms that further use of race in admissions remains unlawful. Second, I agree with the Court's holding that racial discrimination in higher education admissions will be illegal in 25 years. . . . I respectfully dissent from the remainder of the Court's opinion and the judgment, however, because I believe that the Law School's current use of race violates the Equal Protection Clause and that the Constitution means the same thing today as it will in 300 months. . . .

The Constitution abhors classifications based on race, not only because those classifications can harm favored races or are based on illegitimate motives, but also because every time the government places citizens on racial registers and makes race relevant to the provision of burdens or benefits, it demeans us all. "Purchased at the price of immeasurable human suffering, the equal protection principle reflects our Nation's understanding that such classifications ultimately have a destructive impact on the individual and our society." *Adarand Construction, Inc. v. Peña.* . . .

Racial Discrimination Has No Benefits

The absence of any articulated legal principle supporting the majority's principal holding suggests another rationale. I believe what lies beneath the Court's decision today are the benighted notions that one can tell when racial discrimination benefits (rather than hurts) minority groups, . . . and that racial discrimination is necessary to remedy general societal ills. This Court's precedents supposedly settled both issues, but clearly the majority still cannot commit to the principle that racial classifications are *per se* harmful and that almost no amount of benefit in the eye of the beholder can justify such classifications.

Putting aside what I take to be the Court's implicit rejection of *Adarand's* holding that beneficial and burdensome racial classifications are equally invalid, I must contest the notion that the Law School's discrimination benefits those admitted as a result of it. The Court spends considerable time discussing the impressive display of *amicus* support for the Law School in this case from all corners of society. . . . But nowhere in any of the filings in this Court is any evidence that the purported "beneficiaries" of this racial discrimination prove themselves by performing at (or even near) the same level as those students who receive no preferences. . . .

The Purpose of Higher Education

The silence in this case is deafening to those of us who view higher education's purpose as imparting knowledge and skills to students, rather than a communal, rubber-stamp, credentialing process. The Law School is not looking for those students who, despite a lower LSAT score or undergraduate grade point average, will succeed in the study of law. The Law School seeks only a facade—it is sufficient that the class looks right, even if it does not perform right.

Affirmative Action Hurts Black Law Students

Most legal educators have traditionally assumed that [affirmative action] helps blacks by giving them a more elite degree, better connections and maybe even a better education.

But in fact, my data show, about half of black law students end up in the bottom tenth of their classes. Very low grades lead to much higher attrition (blacks are 2½ times more likely to drop out of law school than whites) and to more trouble on the bar exam (blacks are six times as likely as whites taking the bar to never pass).

Richard Sander, "Affirmative Action Hurts Those It's Supposed to Help," Pittsburgh Live.com, January 2, 2005. pittsburghlive.com.

The Law School tantalizes unprepared students with the promise of a University of Michigan degree and all of the opportunities that it offers. These overmatched students take the bait, only to find that they cannot succeed in the cauldron of competition. And this mismatch crisis is not restricted to elite institutions. See T. Sowell, *Race and Culture* 176–177 (1994) ("Even if most minority students are able to meet the normal standards at the 'average' range of colleges and universities, the systematic mismatching of minority students begun at the top can mean that such students are generally overmatched throughout all levels of higher education"). Indeed, to cover the tracks of the aestheticists, this cruel farce of racial discrimination must continue—in selection for the *Michigan Law Review,* see University of Michigan Law School Student Handbook 2002–2003, pp. 39–40 (noting the presence of a "diversity plan" for admission to the review), and in hiring at law firms and for judicial clerkships—until the "beneficiaries" are no longer tolerated. While these students may graduate with law degrees, there is no evidence that they have received a qualitatively better legal education (or become better lawyers) than if they had gone to a less "elite" law school for which they were better prepared. And the aestheticists will never address the real problems facing "underrepresented minorities," instead continuing their social experiments on other people's children.

Stigmatizing Blacks

Beyond the harm the Law School's racial discrimination visits upon its test subjects, no social science has disproved the notion that this discrimination "engender[s] attitudes of superiority or, alternatively, provoke[s] resentment among those who believe that they have been wronged by the government's use of race." *Adarand.* . . . "These programs stamp minorities with a badge of inferiority and may cause them to develop dependencies or to adopt an attitude that they are 'entitled' to preferences." *Ibid.*

It is uncontested that each year, the Law School admits a handful of blacks who would be admitted in the absence of racial discrimination. . . . Who can differentiate between those who belong and those who do not? The majority of blacks are admitted to the Law School because of discrimination, and because of this policy all are tarred as undeserving. This problem of stigma does not depend on determinacy as to whether those stigmatized are actually the "beneficiaries" of racial discrimination. When blacks take positions in the highest places of government, industry, or academia, it is an open question today whether their skin color played a part in their advancement. The question itself is the stigma—because either racial discrimination did play a role, in which case the person may be deemed "otherwise unqualified," or it did not, in which case asking the question itself unfairly marks those blacks who would succeed without discrimination. Is this what the Court means by "visibly open"? . . .

The Gap in Credentials

The Court also holds that racial discrimination in admissions should be given another 25 years before it is deemed no longer narrowly tailored to the Law School's fabricated compelling state interest. . . . While I agree that in 25 years the practices of the Law School will be illegal, they are, for the reasons I have given, illegal now. The majority does not and cannot rest its time limitation on any evidence that the gap in credentials between black and white students is shrinking or will be gone in that timeframe. In recent years there has been virtually no change, for example, in the proportion of law school applicants with LSAT scores of 165 and higher who are black. In 1993 blacks constituted 1.1% of law school applicants in that score range, though they represented 11.1% of all applicants. . . . In 2000 the comparable numbers were 1.0% and 11.3%. . . . No one can seriously contend, and the Court does not, that the racial gap in academic credentials will disappear in 25 years. Nor is the Court's holding that racial discrimination will be unconstitutional in 25 years made contingent on the gap closing in that time.

Indeed, the very existence of racial discrimination of the type practiced by the Law School may impede the narrowing of the LSAT testing gap. An applicant's LSAT score can improve dramatically with preparation, but such preparation is a cost, and there must be sufficient benefits attached to an improved score to justify additional study. Whites scoring between 163 and 167 on the LSAT are routinely rejected by the Law School, and thus whites aspiring to admission at the Law School have every incentive to improve their score to levels above that range. . . . Blacks, on the other hand, are nearly guaranteed admission if they score above 155. . . . As admission prospects approach certainty, there is no incentive for the black applicant to continue to prepare for the LSAT once he is reasonably assured of achieving the requisite score. It is far from certain that the LSAT test-taker's behavior is responsive to the Law School's admissions policies. Nevertheless, the possibility remains that this racial discrimination will help fulfill the bigot's prophecy about black underperformance—just as it confirms the conspiracy theorist's belief that "institutional racism" is at fault for every racial disparity in our society. . . .

For the immediate future, however, the majority has placed its *imprimatur* on a practice that can only weaken the principle of equality embodied in the Declaration of Independence and the Equal Protection Clause. "Our Constitution is color-blind, and neither knows nor tolerates classes among citizens." *Plessy v. Ferguson.* . . . It has been nearly 140 years since Frederick Douglass asked the intellectual ancestors of the Law School to "do nothing with us!" and the Nation adopted the Fourteenth Amendment. Now we must wait another 25 years to see this principle of equality vindicated. I therefore respectfully dissent from the remainder of the Court's opinion and the judgment.

"Diversity . . . when properly implemented, has the potential to enhance many important educational outcomes."

Diversity Improves Education

Mitchell J. Chang

Diversity enhances the educational experience of all students, claims Mitchell J. Chang in the following viewpoint. For all students to reap its benefits, he argues, diversity must be more than an end in itself. While having a diverse population of students is important, Chang asserts that schools must also provide programs that bring students together, encourage dialogue, and give minority students the tools they need to succeed. Chang is an associate professor of education at the University of California, Los Angeles.

As you read, consider the following questions:

1. According to Chang, why does an increase in the proportion of underrepresented students enhance educational opportunities for all students?
2. What aspect of diversity do admissions policies tend to focus on, in the author's view?
3. In the author's opinion, what is compositional diversity?

Mitchell J. Chang, "Reconsidering the Diversity Rationale," *Liberal Education*, Winter 2005. Copyright © 2005 by the Association of American Colleges and Universities. Reproduced by permission.

In recent years, much attention, including my own, has focused on empirically testing diversity's contributions to students' learning and experiences. . . . In a synthesis for the Association of American Colleges and Universities (AAC&U) about diversity-related research, Jeffrey Milem, Anthony Antonio, and I concluded that the social science research generally suggests that, because racial differences are associated with differences in viewpoints and opinions, an increase in the proportion of underrepresented students can bring to a university experiences, outlooks, and ideas that can potentially enhance the educational experiences of all students. The overall educational impact of racial diversity, however, seems to be largely determined by the level of student engagement or involvement, and so the impact is likely to be strongest when campuses intervene by coordinating a set of mutually supportive and reinforcing experiences.

The Benefits Associated with Racial Diversity

Perhaps because admissions policies have been so closely scrutinized and tested, policy makers, educators, litigators, and researchers often look first at composition and examine the statistical results of schools' admissions policies. When the focus is solely or primarily on compositional diversity, however, there is a tendency to treat diversity as an end in itself, rather than as an educational process that, when properly implemented, has the potential to enhance many important educational outcomes.

A study I conducted with several colleagues illustrates this potential. We experimentally tested psychological explanations of the impact of diversity by drawing upon theories of minority influence. Minority influence theories contend that when minority opinions are present in groups, cognitive complexity is stimulated among majority opinion members. We extended the theory to experimentally test whether the presence of diversity in groups also enhances complex thinking. Our findings suggest a positive effect of diversity, particularly when group discussions include an issue with generally different racial viewpoints (e.g., the death penalty). Our experiments also showed that, in these group discussions, minority students cause others to think about the issue in different ways, introduce novel perspectives to the discussion, and are influential in the group. In short, due to the ongoing power of race to shape life experiences in U.S. society, racial and ethnic compositional diversity can create a rich and complex social and learning environment that subsequently can be engaged as an educational tool to promote all students' learning and development.

How Educators Can Really Advance Diversity

Because a student's understanding of and willingness to interact with diversity is not assured, and because both understanding and willingness influence engagement in a robust exchange of ideas, a sustained and coordinated effort regarding diversity is necessary to increase the positive effects on student development and learning. In the synthesis for AAC&U noted earlier, we found that research on diversity consistently shows that educational benefits do not automatically accrue to students who attend institutions that are, in terms of student or faculty composition, racially and ethnically diverse. Rather, if the benefits of diversity in higher education are to be realized, close attention must be paid to the institutional context in which that diversity is enacted. In other words, it is not enough to simply bring together a diverse group of students. Although this is an important first step in creating opportunities for students to learn from diversity, it cannot be the only step that is taken. Diverse college campuses provide unique challenges and opportunities that must be considered if the learning opportunities they present are to be maximized.

Our research synthesis identifies several effective ways to maximize such opportunities for cognitive and personal growth, particularly regarding increases in cultural knowledge and understanding, leadership abilities, and commitment to promoting understanding. Besides bringing diverse students together, campuses must provide stimulating courses covering historical, cultural, and social bases of diversity and community, and they must create additional opportunities and expectations for students to interact across racial and other social differences. Such intentional institutional efforts are critical because it is much easier and less risky for students to gravitate to people of the same racial or ethnic background. When students retreat from the rich and complex social and learning opportunities offered by a diverse campus and settle into institutional spaces that are more homogenous, they are likely to miss out on the important benefits derived from diversity. Hence, there is a behavioral aspect of the institutional context that is important to examine as we consider how students benefit from diversity on campus. More specifically, our AAC&U synthesis points to several key areas often in need of more concentrated intervention: developing outreach, academic enrichment, and recruitment programs; strengthening a college-going culture in the high schools; providing access to a rigorous academic curriculum; providing academic support for college preparation; and retaining students and advancing their academic success.

Transforming Schools

• Students who have experienced positive relationships with culturally different students tend to be more open-minded, develop positive citizenship traits, and experience greater intellectual self-confidence and engagement than students who have not experienced these positive relationships.

• Incorporating a variety of instructional practices and assessments to accommodate a classroom that includes linguistically and culturally diverse students can help those struggling learners who previously may have been labeled slow.

• Transforming school norms and structures to embrace a wider variety of learning styles and cultures can help create a community of successful learners that includes more students than those who previously fit the "ideal" student mold.

Southwest Educational Development Laboratory, "Diversity in Our Schools," *Southwest Educational Development Laboratory Letter*, December 2000. www.sedl.org.

Fundamentally, those interventions begin with concentrated efforts toward remedying the present effects of past racial discrimination. This is necessary to establish the appropriate resources and conditions that drive educational benefits associated with diversity, as well as to facilitate the benefits process. As my UCLA [University of California, Los

Angeles] colleagues and I discuss, admitting underrepresented students is just one part of a comprehensive intervention strategy. Often, more selective campuses also must actively recruit, provide financial support, and compensate for inequities in K-12 education just to yield a significant number of underrepresented students. Likewise, in order to facilitate the benefits process associated with a racially diverse student body, even open-enrollment campuses must find ways to engage underrepresented students both academically and socially, as well as to provide more opportunities for all students to interact freely, wisely, and responsibly with one another. Establishing a campus climate and culture that facilitate those types of student engagement and interaction typically begins with interventions, supported by top-level administrators, that effectively address the vestiges of racism.

Failure to intervene at a basic remedial level not only reduces the chances of realizing the benefits associated with a racially diverse student population but also can fuel racial alienation, antipathy, higher rates of departure, and student dissatisfaction with the overall college experience. This point was underscored in an overlooked brief from student intervenors who charged that the University of Michigan failed to take account of legacies of racial discrimination as reflected in histories of segregated schooling, inequitable admissions requirements, and negative and hostile campus climates for historically underrepresented students. The student intervenors argued that the university failed to intervene in ways that provided underrepresented students with appropriate institutional support and conditions that fostered their intellectual and social development.

Desegregation and Integration

Those who have translated the rhetorical praise of diversity into practice know well that diversity is fundamentally about action—often time consuming and difficult efforts oriented toward remedying the effects of previous exclusions. This work or action toward diversification takes into consideration various levels and dimensions of the campus racial climate and an institution's context in shaping student-learning outcomes. Years of advancing this extraordinary transformation as an educator, researcher, and college administrator have taught me these lessons well. The same lessons have been echoed in many of AAC&U's groundbreaking publications concerning diversity, which offer some of the richest insights by leading scholars addressing this democratic transformation in higher education.

As we come to recognize that diversity is a complex process that must be facilitated by a set of institutional interventions, it is especially helpful to understand better two important distinctions that are not mutually exclusive: desegregation and integration. As Education Professor William Trent once told me, the term desegregation can be understood as mostly a description of demographic shifts occurring within a specific community, whereas integration—not to be confused with assimilation—mostly concerns socio-cultural changes that seek to embrace new members of a community. For example, interventions for addressing desegregation on college campuses might focus mostly on enrolling a diverse student population and keeping them engaged on campus. Achieving this, although difficult and important, is only the beginning of the process. Perhaps even more challenging is addressing integration, which requires changes that tend to be more organic and institution specific. Broadly speaking, interventions that seek to achieve integration will critically examine and address some sacred and difficult issues such as an institution's history of discrimination, the community's range of values, the campus behavioral and psychological climate, and existing programs and initiatives.

Perhaps the types of colleges that deserve our closest attention are those that can be described as desegregated but that are having difficulty with integration, as evidenced by reports of racial antipathy, social segregation, classroom micro-aggression, heightened stereotype threat, curricular narrowness, etc. Such a campus illustrates well that the most interesting aspect of diversity is whether or not there is a certain compositional makeup, but the process communities undergo and how they might intervene strategically to facilitate both desegregation and integration.

In the end, thinking about diversity as a dynamic process rather than as a fixed numerical outcome suggests that the work related to diversity—and very difficult and demanding work at that—is ongoing and ever changing. Political philosopher Stephen Macedo sums it up well: "At its best, talk of diversity . . . reminds us of the extent to which the promise of freedom and equality for all remains a work in progress: only partially realized, only partially understood."

"Diversity in higher education is a lesson in disappointment."

Diversity Does Not Improve Education

Peter Wood

While diversity is one of the most sought after qualities in educational institutions, a diverse student population rarely results in improved cultural awareness among students, argues Peter Wood in the following viewpoint. Racial diversity, he maintains, does not ensure a diversity of perspectives. In fact, Wood contends, programs that promote diversity perpetuate alienation and a sense of grievance among minorities. Wood, who writes for *Partisan Review*, is professor of anthropology at Boston University.

As you read, consider the following questions:
1. According to Wood, what other values are trumped by diversity in colleges and universities?
2. What are the "differences" that the author claims are most prominent at many universities?
3. How does Wood claim that the ideology of diversity frames American history?

D iallo Shabazz received some unexpected attention in September 2000 when the *Daily Cardinal*, the student newspaper at the University of Wisconsin at Madison, discovered his face in a crowd. Well, at least in the photograph of a crowd. Anna Gould, an alert reporter at the *Daily Cardinal*, noticed that in a picture of fans at a football game that adorned a University of Wisconsin brochure, the sun was shining brightly on the face of the one black student in the crowd. The white fans around him were sunless.

It soon came out that University of Wisconsin admissions officials had digitally lifted Mr. Shabazz's face from a 1994 photograph and inserted it into the picture of an all-white crowd at the football game, which in turn went into one hundred thousand copies of the admissions brochure. Shabazz was chosen for no reason other than skin color and the fact that the admissions office had his photograph on file. Caught in their sunny-faced lie, admissions director Rob Seltzer and publications director Al Friedman apologized, and Paul Barrows, vice chancellor for student affairs, said it was "an error in judgment."

Shabazz himself said the incident was "a symptom of a much larger problem," and added, "Diversity on this campus is not really being dealt with." A college senior at the time and a member of the Multicultural Student Coalition, Shabazz seemed to struggle with the incident. The *Milwaukee Journal Sentinel* described him standing before a crowd of 250 students, most white, holding up:

> a copy of an admissions booklet with a new cover featuring a building—and no people.

> "I refuse to believe this is the best we can do to create diversity on this campus," he said. "Institutions don't apologize verbally. Institutions apologize with policy changes and budget changes."

Manipulating Identity

The image of Diallo Shabazz holding up the depopulated brochure and haranguing a little crowd about the need for more and better diversity is the perfect coda to this story. He seems, at last, in accord with Directors Seltzer and Friedman and Vice Chancellor Barrows, who are also on the side of more diversity, and who realize indeed it is not about apologizing "verbally." It is about manipulating identity. And it is about pictures.

Diversity pictures are in fact a well-defined college genre. Most colleges and universities produce viewbooks—infomercials—aimed at high school students, and most of these viewbooks (and many other college publications) include photographs intended to show off the racial and ethnic diversity of the colleges. The University of Wisconsin merely went one step further when it teleported Diallo Shabazz into a crowd of white people.

In January 2002, Mark Hixxon and Kirsten Hubbard, two students at the University of California, San Diego, contributed a three-part feature on "the issue of diversity" to their student newspaper, the *UCSD Guardian*. Their hook for the second part of this report was an analysis of the cover photo for the viewbook, *Discover UCSD*: "Clockwise from the top, there is an Asian female, a South Asian–looking male, a female of undetermined mixed heritage, a Hispanic female, a Caucasian male, a Caucasian female, and an African-American male." Hixxon and Hubbard then point out that the proportions of groups in the photo approximate the Asian, Caucasian and "other" proportions of the actual student body, but the single African-American student misrepresents the reality. Only "1 percent of UCSD's undergraduate body is African-American."

True Believers

The *Discover UCSD* photo is not exactly a lie, but it captures the dubious position of college administrators who are committed to selling diversity to prospective students even if the campus demographics don't match rhetoric. Hixxon and Hubbard focus on this disparity. UCSD, it seems, succeeds in attracting students who like the idea of diversity, but those students are at some risk of being disappointed. Freshman Leila Dingding (her actual name), for example, was attracted to UCSD because "they represented themselves as so diverse." But Miss Dingding has grown skeptical: "Now that I'm actually here, I feel kind of like I was deceived." She adds, "I would feel more comfortable if our school were more diverse," and complains that the summer program before college was more diverse than the actual university.

She is not alone. American grade schools and high schools put enormous effort into instilling in children the doctrine of diversity. In many schools, diversity is unabashedly taught as a higher and better value than equality, freedom, justice and liberty. According to some critics, the focus on diversity in American schools has reached the extreme of undermining instruction in reading and writing. Be that as it may, students like Miss Dingding absorb the main point: Few matters are more important than diversity, and college is where one goes to find it.

College officials are fully aware of this market reality and they respond to it by packaging what they have to offer in the language and the images that they calculate will appeal to seventeen-year-olds. I do not mean to suggest that diversity is merely a marketing tactic for colleges and universities. To the contrary, higher education has many true believers in the doctrine of diversity, and a large penumbra of people who regard diversity as benign and possibly beneficial. Their support, whether strenuous or passive, makes diversity a powerful force on campus.

Simplifications and Falsehoods

But in addition to that, diversity is also a come-on to America's miseducated and uneducated youth, who generally arrive at college believing two or three of diversity's simplifications and falsehoods. The typical college applicant generally accepts, for example, that someone's "perspective" is not gained by study and effort but is rather determined by his or her group membership. The typical college applicant finds nothing amiss in the idea that education is what happens when two or more such "perspectives" are in the same vicinity, and remains convinced that an important reason to attend college is to experience being with people who are "different" from oneself.

Even if the admissions office at a university were under the stewardship of people wise enough to doubt these bits of dogma, it would be risky to publish a viewbook that called into question what the large majority of applicants believe.

Some students might be inspired by the idea that we go to college to overcome the merely local and particular in our social backgrounds and thereby seek a place in a universal culture. A few might catch fire at the idea that differences in perspective are mostly trivial and that education requires the hard effort of examining argument and evidence to decide, as best we can, which account of all we are offered is more nearly *true*. And some might rise to the idea that they have already learned how to tolerate differences, and that college is a place to pursue more advanced lessons in democratic self-government. But chances are that most high school students, indoctrinated for twelve years in the tenets of diversity, would be repelled by such ideas.

Creating Thought-Prisons

It's no surprise that at the same time that American universities have engaged in a serious commitment to diversity, they have been thought-prisons. We are not talking about diversity in any real way. We are talking about brown, black, white versions of the same political ideology. It is very curious that the United States and Canada both assume that diversity means only race and ethnicity. They never assume it might mean more Nazis, or more Southern Baptists. That's diversity too, you know.

Richard Rodriguez, interview by Scott London, *Arts and Opinion*, vol. 3, no. 6, 2004.

In this sense, diversity has closed its circle. Colleges and universities incessantly proclaim their commitment to diversity. Many prospective college students weigh that commitment as a positive factor in deciding where to seek admission and where to enroll. Once enrolled, the students begin to recognize that actual college diversity does not perform according to the theory or the hype. Many students self-segregate into racial and ethnic enclaves in which they acquire a new vocabulary of group rights and generalized resentment. Campus diversity, in practice, seldom turns out to be "inclusive." Rather it is accusatory and divisive. The "differences" that come to the fore are those of students who are aggressive in pushing their agendas aimed at gaining power and privilege, not those of the mostly imaginary ideal of cultural exchange. After being exposed to this for a semester or two, students grow disenchanted. But instead of questioning the premises of diversity itself, the students typically blame the college for not providing enough or the right kinds of diversity. Leila Dingding of UC San Diego concludes: "I would be more comfortable if our school were more diverse. That way, I would experience more cultural awareness and understanding of our diverse society." Like Diallo Shabazz, she does not doubt the theory of diversity, only the practices of her own college.

The Failure of Diversity

In a subtle way, the feeling that the institution has failed to deliver is really part of the theory. Diversity is, after all, an ideology based on rejection of America's oldest and most enduring ideals. It frames American history as a story of callously dominant groups and the groups they dominated, victimizers and victims. As an ideology, it thrives on people feeling shortchanged. Despite the upbeat brochures of different skin tones, diversity can be sustained only to the extent that large numbers of people continue to feel a sense of grievance. And to that end, it supplies its own grievance in the form of making students feel that their colleges perpetually fall short of the goal.

The psychology of diversity thus resembles any number of other movements that cycle their own disappointments back into the original myth. The failures of the Soviet system proved the need for more communism; the sinfulness of the brethren proved the need for more Puritanism; the grumbling of the volcano required another human sacrifice.

Diversity can be understood historically as a way of transforming the supposedly temporary preferences of affirmative action into permanent rights. But as the era in which conspicuous barriers were erected to members of various groups slips further and further into the past, it becomes more and more difficult to justify those privileges. Diversity advocates respond to this difficulty in part by promoting the idea that profound—if mostly invisible—barriers remain. Invoking invisible and often undetectable barriers, however, is a weak way of attempting to persuade others. Building frustration and resentment works better, at least for a while. And it produces profound—if mostly invisible—benefits.

In this sense, the widespread feeling among college students that they have not been rewarded with liberating "cultural awareness"—that their colleges have fallen short—fits with the diversity movement's deeper emotional currents. The promise of personal fulfillment through diversity usually gleams in the distance. Diversity in higher education is a lesson in disappointment.

| *"Affirmative action . . . is really about access to resources and institutions of higher learning in the face of . . . persistent discrimination and economic inequality."*

Affirmative Action Promotes Equal Access to Education

Millery Polyne

Race-based affirmative action helps minorities compete fairly with whites, maintains Millery Polyne in the following viewpoint. Affirmative action, he claims, has been and continues to be necessary to correct racial inequalities. Americans should not let advances achieved through affirmative action lull them into believing that such policies are no longer useful, Polyne asserts. Poor urban schools remain populated by blacks and Latinos, who remain underrepresented at elite colleges and universities. Polyne is assistant professor of humanities at City University of New York, Staten Island.

As you read, consider the following questions:

1. According to Polyne, how do affirmative action opponents justify their opinion that such policies are no longer necessary?
2. From what sorts of affirmative action have whites traditionally benefited, in the author's view?
3. In the author's opinion, what percentage of the student body do blacks comprise at the country's prominent colleges and universities?

Pictured on the cover of the January 27, 2003 issue of *Newsweek* was a handsome young black man dressed in a crisp IBM-esque navy blue shirt and power red tie strategically fitted at the base of his leather belt. Clean-shaven, designer eyewear and khaki pants present his image as the poster child for middle-class black America—striving, upwardly mobile and assimilationist. Coupled with this black male image which represented a tolerant and progressive America, the *Newsweek* headline read: "Do We Still Need Affirmative Action?" The question and this image became a permanent fixture in my gallery of thoughts for weeks. The black man on the cover resembled a myriad of young men that I had the privilege of studying with at Morehouse College, intelligent men who came from both working and middle-class homes, and both poor and selective schools. However, a well-groomed African American does not alone represent the beneficiaries of affirmative action. Black faces proliferate the airwaves of prime time media shows and are displayed on the covers of magazines and newspaper articles. Is it not critical to also consider how white women and non-blacks benefit from affirmative action policy?

Imprisoned in a Racist Box

African America has been situated at the center of this conservative affirmative action debate in such a way that black intelligence and black ability continues to be imprisoned in a racist box of doubt and inferiority. This focus on African Americans (no longer the largest minority ethnic group in the U.S.) and the indifference paid to advantages gained by white women and other underrepresented groups further polarizes race relations in the U.S. and impedes the development of a multiracial democracy.

The *Newsweek* cover underscored heated debates on the University of Michigan's campus. As a recent graduate of the doctoral program in History, I participated and watched rallies on the Diag[1] and mediated discussions in my classroom as a graduate student instructor. Attempts to place the land-

---

1. a green lawn on the University of Michigan campus

mark *Bakke*[2] case of 1978 in its proper context of civil rights struggles, racial and gender prejudices and the legacy of white-male supremacy were duly noted by students, but quickly disregarded as they asserted the particular advancements of people of color and women since the 1970s and argued how U.S. race relations have changed for the better. The U.S. has changed—there is a more visible black middle-class, there are African Americans as CEOs of Fortune 500 companies—and Oprah is a billionaire. Apparently, the relative gains of the Civil Rights Movement among people of color and women prove that affirmative action has run its course, that it legally violates the rights of others (i.e., whites), and that it obstructs the existence and success of a meritocratic and color-blind society. As George Lipsitz, Ethnic Studies Professor at University of California, San Diego, argues: "It is a mistake to posit a gradual and inevitable trajectory of evolutionary progress in race relations . . ." because battles have been won and lost, before and after civil rights legislation, for social and economic justice. These hard fought protests vividly illustrate that race, class and gender inequality remain a significant deterrent to social progress in the U.S. Nevertheless, an illusion of a colorblind and egalitarian order in the U.S. persists, but the defense of affirmative action by the Supreme Court disturbs that fantasy.

One's illusions that race and gender are no longer central factors to one's access to resources and to upward mobility help silence major issues critical to the affirmative action debate. For example, as race is pushed to the center of university admissions policy, the discussion of legacy, a provost's discretion in admissions, scholarship athletes and even faculty spousal hires are swiftly marginalized. Some of these factors directly support institutional development, but also give preference to those meeting certain financial, physical or familial criteria. Historically, middle-class and wealthy whites have benefited from such considerations, capitalizing on the rewards of whiteness and leveraging their business and social contacts among white elites. James M. McPher-

2. *University of California v. Bakke*, 1978: A Supreme Court ruling permitting the use of race as one factor in college admission

son, noted Princeton historian and president of the American Historical Association, affirmed the existence of an "old boy network"[3] that solidified educational and job opportunities for whites. In 1962, McPherson asserted that Princeton "offered me the job (a faculty position), without a real interview and without having seen any dissertation chapters." In addition, McPherson did not recall if his thesis advisor, C. Vann Woodward, even put his recommendation "in writing." "This was the infamous 'old boy network'" McPherson argued, "surely the most powerful instrument of affirmative action ever devised." By no means have I suggested that the current affirmative action policy be designed similar to that described in McPherson's case or that it supports the above behavior. However, McPherson's tenure at Princeton is a symbol of the legacy of white privilege and preference that has hindered black advancement in the U.S.

Restricted Opportunities

Moreover, poor urban schools, where black and Latino students attend disproportionately, have been detrimental to their educational progress. Supporters and opponents of affirmative action both agree that educational spending in urban, suburban and rural districts needs to be more equitably distributed in order for students of color to succeed in the national and international marketplace. However, since school earnings depend largely on property taxes, would the middle-class and wealthy (of any ethnic background) be willing to pay more taxes in order to level the financial playing field of U.S. schools? Unlikely. It is clear that during this neoconservative presidency [of George W. Bush] where the government's commitment to social services and education is dwindling, the economy is suffering and unemployment is at its highest in recent memory, only those persons with a solid financial and educational foundation (also a strong personal network) will be able to make significant strides in this society. Subsequently, upward mobility and opportunity are restricted to those with wealth and influence.

A study by the Educational Testing Service (ETS) reveals

3. an informal, exclusive system of mutual assistance in which favors are exchanged

that a majority of students attending prominent colleges and universities come from middle-class and wealthy families. According to the ETS, 74 percent of students at 146 elite institutions come from the top 25 percent of the nation's socio-economic levels. 3 percent of students come from the bottom 25 percent. However, at these schools there remains a consistent percentage of black faces at less than 8 percent. As Cornel West has asserted, this is "far from a takeover." Yet the media and neoconservatives tend to focus on blacks as if they were the only ones benefiting from this admissions policy. Thus, within the prestigious walls of the academy diversity equates to variations within the bourgeoisie and elites. Furthermore, since neoconservatives have framed the anti-affirmative action debate "diversity" and "multiculturalism" are now disparaging code words for handouts and inferior students of color. African Americans and Latinos are encaged within a racist and unfair paradigm where nothing but test scores are indicators of merit, potential and the subjective world of success.

What Happens Without Affirmative Action?

• Following the University of California Regents' decision to eliminate race and ethnicity as one of many factors to consider in admissions decisions, the Berkeley campus experienced a 55-percent drop in minority admissions, while the Los Angeles campus experienced a 36-percent decline.

• In 1997, African American student enrollment in the Texas public medical schools dropped 54 percent, and among California's medical schools, the enrollment of underrepresented minorities declined 32 percent in 1998 from its peak in the mid-1990s.

American Psychological Association, "How Affirmative Action Benefits America," APA Web site, August 1999. www.apa.org.

Colorblind perspectives overshadow an extraordinarily color conscious world and render American social and political space uncritical of racist thought and practices. During the affirmative action debate the intellectual capabilities of people of African descent are again up for question in the public arena. It has become disturbingly reminiscent of the legacy of scientific racism rooted in the nineteenth and early twentieth century. Black intelligence should not be the issue. Black people will continue to excel in spite of racism. However, poor schools, unequal distribution of wealth, increasing numbers of black and brown men and women filling up prison industrial complexes serve as a stronger argument to explain lagging test scores. The affirmative action issue is really about access to resources and institutions of higher learning in the face of a struggling economy, a neoconservative backlash, and persistent discrimination and economic inequality against non-whites. Providing legitimate educational and financial opportunities to those in need serves as a stepping stone to ameliorating race relations in our communities.

Still in Its Early Stages

After twenty-five years affirmative action is still in its early stages. Admittedly, it has flaws, but those shortcomings mirror a society that has yet to adequately address the issues of racial slavery and white privilege. The U.S. Supreme Court ruling in June 2003 was indeed a watershed moment. Its decision in favor of diversity as a viable factor in the admissions process at public institutions acknowledges that inequality exists along racial lines. In addition, the verdict sets the stage for critical action against the insidiousness of white supremacy and the affirmation of a multiracial democracy. Yet, the Court's ruling also denounced the University of Michigan's point system and did not overthrow the law against the use of race in admissions in the states of Washington and California. The elimination of a point system, which documents the admissions process and maintains accountability, allows for even more subjectivity and a return to elite and white privilege in school admissions. We cannot allow that to happen if we as Americans deem intolerance of all kinds an obstacle to progress.

Race and racism has been part of the social fabric of the U.S. ever since Africans were brought to this shore. But to showcase people of color, particularly blacks, in a debate that no longer means opportunity but inferiority is certainly not the road to revisit. Exploring and critiquing the literature on whiteness opens new doors to this discussion and poses new questions to the current debate that has America spinning its wheels. As George Lipsitz asserts: "whiteness is invested in, like property . . . [it provides people] with resources, power and opportunity." Our investment in whiteness, regardless of race or ethnicity, continues to be one of society's major impediments to achieving social justice. Optimistically, Justice Sandra Day O'Connor envisions a world twenty-five years from now where those hurdles will be removed for all, despite hundreds of years of race, gender and economic struggle. But, if we intend to achieve such a feat, disinvestment in whiteness must begin today.

"Race-based affirmative action . . . is a kind of collective bribe rich people pay themselves for ignoring economic inequality."

Affirmative Action Does Not Promote Equal Access to Education

Walter Benn Michaels

While affirmative action has traditionally been seen as a way to secure equal opportunities for women and minorities, in the following viewpoint Walter Benn Michaels claims that it has failed to provide equal access to education. Many campuses, Michaels argues, are racially integrated, but socio-economically homogenous. Indeed, he maintains, those who come from poor backgrounds remain underrepresented and face the greatest educational obstacles. According to Michaels, programs that helped the poor would do more good than affirmative action. Michaels is associate professor of English at the University of California, Berkeley.

As you read, consider the following questions:

1. According to Michaels, what code words do Americans use to refer to race?
2. What percentage of Harvard undergraduates come from families with annual incomes of more than $80,000, in the author's opinion?
3. In the author's view, why is diversity a rich people's problem?

The university where I [teach]—the University of Illinois, Chicago [U.I.C.]—is a large, increasingly underfinanced public university. Our classrooms are overcrowded. Our physical plant is deteriorating. Many departments cannot afford to hire any new professors.

But as we, like other universities around the country, send out our final admissions letters [in April 2004], there is at least one bright spot, one area where we have done well and are poised to do even better. Seemingly every piece of literature that U.I.C. distributes about itself announces that we have been "ranked among the Top 10 universities in the country for the diversity" of "our student body." And that diversity, the literature goes on to point out, "is one of the greatest aspects of our campus." The bad news about our current condition is that you may be jammed into a classroom so full that you can't find a place to sit. But the good news is that 46 percent of the people jammed in there with you will be Caucasian, 21 percent will be Asian, 13 percent will be Hispanic and 9 percent will be African-American.

It is often said that Americans don't like to talk about race, but no remark is more false. The eagerness of other schools to produce their own versions of U.I.C.'s diversity figures makes it obvious that, in fact, we love to talk about race. And we not only talk about it, we also write books about it, we teach classes about it and we arrange our admissions policies to take it into account.

A Collective Fantasy

It is true, however, that we don't so much like to call it race. Students, faculty members and administrators often prefer to speak of their cultural identities. Unimpressed by the objection that—speaking the same language, wearing the same clothes, reading the same books—they all seem to me to belong to the same culture, my students speak proudly of their own cultures and respectfully of others'. Some might be taller than others, some might be smarter than others, some might be better-looking than others, but all belong to cultures, and all the cultures are worthy of respect. And that's the advantage of the idea of culture: it gives us a world of differences without inequality.

145

And the enthusiasm for such differences is widespread. When I asked a group of Harvard literature students about what distinguished them from a parallel group of literature students at U.I.C., they were prepared to acknowledge that the U.I.C. students might be even more diverse than they were, but they were unable to see the relevance of the fact that the U.I.C. group was also less wealthy. And this is equally true of the students at U.I.C. who identify themselves as black, white, Arab, Asian and Hispanic and not as poor or working class. After all, your ethnicity is something you can be proud of in a way that your poverty or even your wealth (since it's your parents' wealth) is not.

But the real value of diversity is not primarily in the contribution it makes to students' self-esteem. Its real value is in the contribution it makes to the collective fantasy that institutions ranging from U.I.C. to Harvard are meritocracies that reward individuals for their own efforts and abilities—as opposed to rewarding them for the advantages of their birth. For if we find that the students at an elite university like Harvard or Yale are almost as diverse as the students at U.I.C., then we know that no student is being kept from a Harvard because of his or her culture. And white students can understand themselves to be there on merit because they didn't get there at the expense of black people.

A Rich People's Problem

We are often reminded of how white our classrooms would look if we did away with affirmative action. But imagine what Harvard would look like if instead we replaced race-based affirmative action with a strong dose of class-based affirmative action. Ninety percent of the undergraduates come from families earning more than $42,000 a year (the median household income in the U.S.)—and some 77 percent come from families with incomes of more than $80,000, although only about 20 percent of American households have incomes that high. If the income distribution at Harvard were made to look like the income distribution of the United States, some 57 percent of the displaced students would be rich, and most of them would be white. It's no wonder that many rich white kids and their parents seem to like diversity. Race-based affirmative action, from this standpoint, is a kind of collective bribe rich people pay themselves for ignoring economic inequality. The fact (and it is a fact) that it doesn't help to be white to get into Harvard replaces the much more fundamental fact that it does help to be rich and that it's virtually essential not to be poor.

The Color of Privilege

I believe that the color that gives you the most advantage in this country is green. Skin color is incomparable to financial wealth. Families with more money have more advantage, regardless of one's skin pigmentation. Affirmative action policy should be changed to help only those who come from low-income families, because those families are most deserving. Socioeconomic affirmative action is race-blind, so it would eliminate using reverse racism to select people. The credibility of those aided by socioeconomic affirmative action would not be constantly challenged, as many current minority students are, because family income usually remains private information.

Andy Clavin, "Clashing Campus Viewpoints: Race-Based Affirmative Action Does More Harm than Good," *Stanford Daily Online*, July 10, 2003. http://daily.stanford.edu.

Hence the irrelevance of Harvard's recent announcement that it won't ask parents who earn less than $40,000 a year to help pay for their children's education. While this is no doubt great news to those financially pressed students who have gone to great schools, taken college-prep courses and scored well on their SAT's, it's bound to seem a little beside the point to the great majority of the poor, since what's keeping them out of elite universities is not their inability to pay the bill but their inability to qualify for admission in the first place.

In the end, we like policies like affirmative action not so much because they solve the problem of racism but because they tell us that racism is the problem we need to solve. And the reason we like the problem of racism is that solving it just requires us to give up our prejudices, whereas solving the problem of economic inequality might require something more—it might require us to give up our money. It's not surprising that universities of the upper middle class should want their students to feel comfortable. What is surprising is that diversity should have become the hallmark of liberalism.

This, if you're on the right, is the gratifying thing about campus radicalism. When student and faculty activists struggle for cultural diversity, they are in large part battling over what skin color the rich kids should have. Diversity, like gout, is a rich people's problem. And it is also a rich people's solution. For as long as we're committed to thinking of difference as something that should be respected, we don't have to worry about it as something that should be eliminated. As long as we think that our best universities are fair if they are appropriately diverse, we don't have to worry that most people can't go to them, while others get to do so because they've had the good luck to be born into relatively wealthy families. In other words, as long as the left continues to worry about diversity, the right won't have to worry about inequality.

Periodical Bibliography

The following articles have been selected to supplement the diverse views presented in this chapter.

Sam Berns	"Let Affirmative Action Work Now so It Is," *Daily Cardinal*, February 4, 2003.
Christian Science Monitor	"A Better Path to Diversity," April 11, 2000.
Henry Louis Gates Jr.	"Breaking the Silence," *New York Times*, August 1, 2004.
Jaime Glazov	"The End of Blackness," *FrontPageMagazine. com*, February 20, 2004. www.frontpagemag. com/Articles/ReadArticle.asp?ID=12273.
Lino A. Graglia	"Winks, Nods—and Preferences," *Wall Street Journal*, June 25, 2003.
Ben Jackson	"The Other Candidate," *Chronicle of Higher Education*, July 2, 2003.
Jeff Jacoby	"On Flattering Minorities," *Townhall.com*, March 19, 2004. www.townhall.com/ columnist/jeffjacoby/jj20040319.shtml.
Neal Kumar Katyal	"Why Affirmative Action in American Colleges and Universities Should Be Constitutional," *Journal of Blacks in Higher Education*, April 30, 2003.
Marable Manning	"The Death of Affirmative Action," *Jackson Advocate*, May 20–26, 2004.
Jeffrey Rosen	"How I Learned to Love Quotas," *New York Times*, June 1, 2003.
Peter Schwartz	"The Racism of Diversity," Ayn Rand Institute, December 11, 2003. www.aynrand.org/site/ News2?page=NewsArticle&id=7915&news_iv_ ctrl=1076.
Susan Sturm and Lani Guinier	"The Future of Affirmative Action," *Boston Review*, January 2001.
Sean Turner	"Affirmative Action Hurts Historically Black Colleges and Universities," National Center for Public Policy Research, August 2003. www.nationalcenter.org/P21NVTurnerHBCU 803.html.

CHAPTER 4

How Should Society View Interracial Families?

Chapter Preface

During the 2000 presidential elections, a campaign stop by George W. Bush at Bob Jones University in South Carolina touched off a media storm. Bush was widely criticized for appearing at the school, which has a ban on interracial dating, and the school itself became the focus of media attention. Bob Jones III, the school's president, came out soon after the story broke and reversed the ban, which had been in effect for more than fifty years. The policy "is meaningless to us," Jones said in a statement to the media. "The principle upon which it was based is very important," Jones maintains, "but the rule is not. So we did away with it." University officials never made clear the nature of the principle behind the rule but implied that a ban on interracial dating was not in their view wrong, simply immaterial. Despite the ban's reversal, many in the press and the general public were outraged. According to U.S. senator Patrick Leahy, "Bob Jones University has become a symbol of divisiveness and intolerance in our society." Bush himself later expressed regret that he had not spoken out sooner and maintained that the school had done the right thing by reversing the ban.

That a ban on interracial dating would instigate such shock and disapproval on a national level is a sign of how much things have changed in the past few decades. Since the legal prohibition on interracial marriage was struck down in 1967 by the Supreme Court in *Loving v. Virginia*, rates of interracial marriage have risen, and interracial families have gained social acceptance. Beginning in the 1990s, mixed race people were highlighted in numerous media campaigns and advertisements. Tiger Woods, the self-defined "Cablinasian" golf player, became a sort of unofficial avatar of the new mixed-race America. In 2000 *Newsweek* ran a special report on "the new face of race," exploring the ever-increasing subtleties and nuances resulting from the increasing blending of the races in the United States.

The experiences of many Americans, however, lie somewhere between Benetton ad idealism, in which people of all races are united and represented equally, and Bob Jones–style segregation. Interracial families still face prejudice and disapproval, both from within their extended families and from society at large. It is not necessarily whites or conservatives such as Bob Jones who are most likely to oppose interracial marriage. Many of those who are most skeptical of the practice are themselves minorities who worry about what is lost in terms of cultural and racial identity. The mingling of genes, these skeptics worry, cannot overcome centuries of discrimination.

The United States has a long, complicated, and often painful history when it comes to issues of interracial families. The authors of the viewpoints in this chapter consider the varied realities facing interracial families today. They delve into disputes that are frequently simplified in news headlines, and debate how society should respond to interracial families.

"If the rate of inter-racial marriages increases, the next generation may well not identify as 'black' or 'white' at all."

Interracial Marriage Should Be Encouraged

Andrew Sullivan

The interracial marriage rate in the United States is rising, and, argues Andrew Sullivan in the following viewpoint, this increase bodes well for American race relations. This change is particularly evident among black women, who are experiencing economic and social progress, he claims. Because historical taboos against interracial marriage reflect America's racial divide, an increase in interracial marriage, Sullivan asserts, is evidence that rigid racial categories and stereotypes are dissolving. Sullivan is a contributing writer for *New York Times Magazine* and senior editor of the *New Republic*.

As you read, consider the following questions:

1. What landmark U.S. Supreme Court case struck down the ban on interracial marriage?
2. What does Sullivan claim was the number of marriages between black women and white men in 1960?
3. What was the number of such marriages in 2000?

In the long and tortured racial history of America, there have been few more tortured subjects than inter-racial sex. From earliest times, when Thomas Jefferson had an illicit love affair with a slave, the subject has been oddly taboo. Fear of black male sexuality—and white men's sexual insecurity in comparison—powered some of the most racist thuggery of the past. Many lynchings of black men were occasioned by claims of sex with white women, and formal laws banning inter-racial marriage date back to the 1660s. In fact, it wasn't until 1967—a mere thirty-five years ago—that the U.S. Supreme Court, in the wonderfully named case *Loving vs Virginia*, struck down such miscegenation bans throughout the United States. Thirty-five years out of over three hundred is not a long time.

Maintaining White Supremacy

And the bans on such marriages were not arid or legal affairs. They became, in some respects, the most powerful of all laws maintaining white supremacy in the United States. To give a flavor of the feelings aroused by such matters, here's part of the Tennessee state supreme court's judgment in the late nineteenth century, refusing to recognize a marriage between a white man and a black woman. If such a marriage were allowed to stand, the court reasoned, "we might have in Tennessee the father living with his daughter, the son with the mother, the brother with his sister, in lawful wedlock . . . the Turk or the Mohammedan, with his numerous wives, may establish his harem at the doors of the capitol, and we are without remedy. Yet none of these are more revolting, more to be avoided, or more unnatural than the case before us."

There you have it: worse than incest or polygamy. To some early Americans, inter-racial marriage was even worse than bestiality. And the marriage ban also lay behind many of the other institutions of American apartheid. I remember talking to the Southern father of a friend of mine who had grown up in the 1960s and attended the first integrated school in his small Southern town. I asked his father why there was such resistance to integration: "Well," he replied, "it was a mixture of things. Politics—and worrying about your children's education and so on. But the thing people were most worried about was not integrating the schools as such—or the quality of the education. . . . They were worried that once they started integrating the schools, the kids would get to know one another better; and then maybe some of them would get married. That's what they were really worried about." No wonder the U.S. military and schools were integrated and public segregation abolished long before the marriage taboo fell.

Terrific News

All that is a preamble to some terrific news. After decades of very modest rates of interracial marriage in America, the proportion of black women marrying white men has just experienced a dramatic jump. The *Atlanta Journal and Constitution* reported [in July 2002] that, after an annual rate of 26,000 such marriages a year in 1960 and a stable 27,000 in 1980, the number of marriages between black women and white men soared to 80,000 in 2000. This coincides with other encouraging data from teenage black women as well: their pregnancy rates have just hit their lowest level since 1976. And in the latest survey of sexual activity among high-schoolers, the percentage of black teens saying they'd had sex in the last three months dropped from 50 to 40 percent in one year. Whites saw a much smaller decline—from 35 to 32 percent, while Hispanics saw a small rise to 35 percent.

Slowly but surely, black American women are making it. At least that's one plausible explanation for the sudden jump in inter-racial marriage. Women make up over 60 percent of black college degrees. They have more self-confidence, more independence and decreasingly see themselves as trapped in any particular identity, or required because of their skin color to marry one particular race rather than another. The most obvious examples of black female success are Oprah Winfrey—one of the most accomplished business executives around—and Condi Rice, arguably the most powerful woman in the history of American foreign policy (and, yes, I'm including Madeleine Albright in that list). In popular culture, the movies are also beginning to feature more black women dating white men: Halle Berry just won an Oscar for her role dating a white man in "Monster's Ball," and Angela Bassett was Robert de Niro's girlfriend in "The Score."

Youth Lead the Way in Intermarriage

Look at the ratio of both-black marriages to mixed-black marriages in 1990: For those over 65 years of age, the ratio is over 6:1, for those under 35 years old it drops to 3:2, and for those under 25 it approaches 1:1. In 1990, 84% of all married black people over the age of 65 were in both-black marriages, but only 53% of married blacks under 25 were. . . .

Is intermarriage—perhaps the most tangible social marker of tolerance and race-blindness—the province of the educated and the well-to-do? Maybe, but the numbers indicate that generation is the key. And youth is leading the way.

"Can Interracial Marriage Make You Smarter and Richer?" *Stats*, August 1, 1997.

The reasons for the racial break-out are hard to nail down. Part of it may well be the impact of three decades of affirmative action in which black women were increasingly integrated into white work-settings. Interaction on the job led to dates which led to relationships. Then there's the effect of welfare reform. Since the reform took national effect in 1996—against fierce resistance from the left—black women have seen their incomes increase, their pregnancy rates decline, and their family structures solidify. A woman with a job and self-confidence is far more likely to take the risk of dating across the racial barrier than someone trapped in the culture of welfare dependency. These women, unsurprisingly, are also more attractive to men of all races.

The Ultimate Solution

Sadly, the new numbers may also be a function of the dearth of black men to date. With much of the young black male population in jail or in some part of the criminal justice system, there's a huge surplus of datable black women. The remaining black men, according to many black women, know they can pick and choose and enjoy the game itself. One black woman told the Atlanta paper, "I've just found that there is a lack of appreciation of black women in Atlanta. We come a dime a dozen here. I haven't found any black men trying to take me to the museum. I wish they would make an effort other than, 'Let's go and have a drink' or 'Let's go to the Red Lobster for all-you-can-eat crab legs on Monday.'" Into that demographic gap, white men have jumped.

But the real promise lies in the future. If the rate of inter-racial marriage increases, the next generation may well not identify as "black" or "white" at all. That's a real fillip. Miscegenation has always been the ultimate solution to America's racial divisions. It blurs distinctions in the only way in which history can be definitively left behind. It was an interesting coincidence that the week in which the *Atlanta Constitution* ran its article on inter-racial marriage, a new proposition made it onto California's ballot in November [2002]. It's called the Racial Privacy Initiative, and it would forbid the government from asking any citizens about their racial identity. It's an attempt to accelerate the slow decline of fixed racial categories in a new and brownish America. And it captures a growing cultural mood. The comedian Chris Rock has noted that things are really changing in America when the best rapper is white and the best golfer is black. But what's more salient is that neither Eminem nor Tiger Woods sees himself as racially defined or restricted. That's the future. And black women are now helping to bring it about.

"Even as an increasing number of folks of color find love and companionship outside our community, it's a luxury we simply can't afford."

Interracial Relationships Should Be Discouraged

Lakshmi Chaudhry

To avoid frustration, self-loathing, and anger, people of color should be discouraged from entering into interracial romantic relationships, claims Lakshmi Chaudhry in the following viewpoint. In a world where individuals are defined by race, interracial relationships involve more than simple romantic chemistry, she maintains. For example, white men who seek out Asian women often do so because they believe them to be submissive or exotic, she maintains. In fact, Chaudhry contends, rather than transcending stereotypes, mixed-race relationships often end up reinforcing them. Chaudhry is a senior editor of AlterNet, an independent, alternative online newsmagazine.

As you read, consider the following questions:

1. According to Chaudhry, how does popular culture regard Asian men?
2. What is the "price tag" for Asian women who date whites, in the author's opinion?
3. Why do people assume Chaudhry has had an arranged marriage?

"We're at the bottom of the pile, right along with black women," said the young Taiwanese-American, his face red with frustration. He was speaking out at a local dinner/discussion event titled "Mating and Dating in the Asian American Community." The rage among the men in that room was palpable as they spoke of a lifetime of sexual invisibility in a culture that constructs them as either effeminate or repulsive.

A Racial Hierarchy

The sexual marketplace is a minefield for people of color. Our choice of bed partners is defined by a racial hierarchy that places Anglos squarely at the top. They determine who's hot and who's not for the rest of us. Asian men, unfortunately, just don't cut it. Like the geeky Long Duck Dong who chases afar a horrified Molly Ringwald in [the 1984 movie] "Sixteen Candles," popular culture regards them as sexual untouchables. No wonder then that so many of my Asian girlfriends grew up lusting after white guys.

"I wanted to be blonde and beautiful. And this was the closest I was going to get," says Meena, an Indian-American. The thought of being further "raced" by going out with fellow Indians was intolerable.

No Women for the Asian Guy

Hollywood reinforces this desire for assimilation by consistently pairing Asian women with Anglo men. While the very sexy Jet Li is not allowed to kiss Bridget Fonda in "Kiss of the Dragon," celluloid Asian babes can't wait to get their clothes off for the dashing white hero. In "Shanghai Knights," actress Fann Wong is matched up with Owen Wilson instead of Jackie Chang, who is conveniently cast as her brother. Hollywood's message is unmistakable: No women for the Asian guy.

Henry, who is part Chinese and part white, points out that the stereotypes have real-life consequences for the sexual life of an Asian American male. "It means a lot of loneliness. A lot of Friday nights without a date," he says. But Asian men are no less Anglo-centric in their sexual preferences. Author David Mura writes openly of his "rampant promiscuity with white women and an obsession with pornography." Like my friends, he was running as far away as he could from his Asian-ness.

Who Marries Whom?

Interracial couples' husband-wife proportions differ dramatically by race.

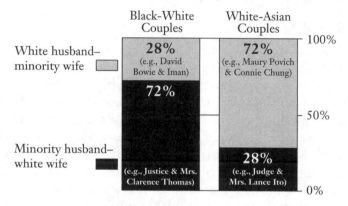

1990 Census, cited in Steve Sailor, *National Review*, July 14, 1997.

The difference, however, is that Asian women have a much better shot at getting some white booty. Sexual objectification has its benefits. Henry calls it "cultural leverage." In other words, thanks to our exotic status, women like me can choose from a broad palette of sexual options. The men in my community want the right to do the same. Therefore their desire for more movies like the newly released, "The Guru," in which Indian actor Jimi Mistry has both Marisa Tomei and Heather Graham fawning over him. The logic is simple: If an Anglo finds you hot, the rest will follow.

Not Choosing the "White" Option

Sounds like a great plan, except that sexual seal of approval may get you more dates, but often comes with a price tag. My Thai friend Susan still fumes over an ad looking for Asian women, which said, "American-born feminists need not apply." The situation within the gay community isn't much better. "Rice queens" (white men with a taste for the Oriental) expect Asian men to play the role of the submissive "bottom." Asians, both male and female, have social capital in our culture, but mostly as docile sex objects.

So it isn't surprising that many of my friends now choose not to exercise their "white" option. The same women who grew up fantasizing about the blonde, blue-eyed stud changed their mind in their 20s. Some combination of personal experience and race consciousness flipped their sexual desire on its head.

"Even if I look at some white guy and think he's cute, I immediately push it aside. I feel like he's never going to really get me," says Nina, a Chinese-American writer. Now she is willing to date any one but an Anglo. Susan gets downright paranoid when she is out with her white gay friend. She chortles, "You're going to think I'm crazy, but I feel like getting up and shouting, 'I'm not his girlfriend?'" Even women who have loving white partners have to worry about how they "look" to others, and often find themselves labeled as sellouts.

A Luxury Many Cannot Afford

Compared to my friends, my childhood in India was relatively sheltered from the harsher realities of race. I spent my teen years falling in and out of love with a number of seriously cute Indian boys. Sure, I had a nauseating crush on Sting, but there was no real prospect of a multiracial romance in my all-Indian world. I could afford to be absurdly naive. My bubble finally burst when an acquaintance suggested—unfairly, I think—that my Kiwi boyfriend in graduate school might have a taste for the exotic.

But even after a decade in this country, I was still taken by surprise when the first white person asked me if I'd had an arranged marriage—all because I'd mentioned that my husband was Indian. It's taken me a long time to understand that in America, my sexual choices are indelibly raced.

A chirpy white woman I once met at an airport lounge said to me, "I don't care about race when it comes to dating. It's all about chemistry." Smug in her liberal credentials, she didn't understand that color-blind attraction is a racial privilege. Even as an increasing number of folks of color find love and companionship outside our community, it's a luxury we simply can't afford. Whomever we love—and of whatever hue or ethnicity—our desire has to run a treacherous course fraught with fear, self-hatred and anger.

In a world still defined by racial divisions, there is no such thing as just plain old chemistry.

"*Sometimes my skin feels as if it wants to burst into flames. Sometimes I wish it were a coat I could take off.*"

Biracial Identity Can Be a Source of Conflict

Shara McCallum

In the following viewpoint Shara McCallum describes the conflict she sometimes experiences as a mixed-race person of African, Indian, European, and Jewish descent. Since she is light-skinned, McCallum maintains, she has always felt a conflict between how she defines herself and how others see her. She claims that she struggles against whiteness, as it stands for oppression and privilege, yet she realizes that her ancestry includes both black and white, both slave and master. McCallum, a poet, lives in Memphis, Tennessee, and teaches at the University of Memphis.

As you read, consider the following questions:

1. What is the adjustment that McCallum faces when she immigrates to the United States?
2. What is the dilemma that McCallum faces when she meets someone who does not know her race?
3. What is "passing," and how does it differ from race, in the author's view?

Shara McCallum, "Snapshots in Black and White," *Creative Nonfiction*, 2002, pp. 67–70. Copyright © 2002 by the Creative Nonfiction Foundation. All rights reserved. Reproduced by permission.

My father died when I was 9 years old, the same year my three sisters and my mother moved with our mother's parents to America, to Miami. He was mixed: African, Indian, European (from Scotland and England), Jewish and we don't know what else. He had schizophrenia. Schizophrenia, a metaphor for multiple selves.

What I remember of my father are fragments. I see him with his guitar. I see him singing and strumming his guitar. I see myself next to him in the gully in his mother's back yard with him playing and singing to me. I see him frozen on a busy street in Kingston: catatonic. I see him cursing and screaming and hitting my mother: paranoid, delusional. I see him crying at his reflection in the mirror.

My father was a Rastafarian for the last 10 years of his life, and my three sisters and I, born in Jamaica, were raised as Rastas, too. My mother tells me that, as a youth, my father went to England and later studied Buddhism before coming to Rastafari, in attempts to understand who he was. By the end of his life, though, he considered himself a black man, she says. "He had gone deep into himself to reach that point and make himself whole." Whole. Schizophrenia. My father tried to commit suicide many times. He succeeded at 33. Schizophrenia is not a metaphor. Race is not a metaphor.

An Uncomfortable Moment

The first time I meet anyone who has known me before seeing me is always the most difficult and uncomfortable moment for each of us: editors who have published my work, someone who has seen my resumé without a picture. The usual blank stare for a moment. The stuttering "*You* are Shara McCallum."

For many years, in part to avoid this sting, in part out of fear of going against the grain, of rocking the boat, I checked "Other" or wrote "mixed" and listed the four continents to which I can lay claim within the span of two generations. A mutt. Mulatta. High yella. Miscegenated. Mixed breed. A dog. A nectarine.

As a child in Jamaica, I was not oblivious to color. I knew I had white or bright or light skin while others had brown and yellow and beige and red and black—cool brown, doo-doo brown, light as light, cream with a dash of coffee, coffee with a dash of cream, reds, lick of the tar brush, coal black, black as night. But I did not understand the usual intersections of color and race. When we came to America, I didn't know that I was black or white. I was 9 and trying to be like the other kids, trying to lose my accent and sound American, trying to catch up on TV shows I'd missed since we didn't have a TV back home in Jamaica, trying to learn to play with Barbie dolls when before I had cooked and cleaned for my younger sisters, trying to learn to wear Chic jeans and feel chic after not having been allowed to wear pants up to that point in my life. I didn't know I was black until my grandmother, my mother's mother, told me, "No one would ever know you are. Only your hair might give you away." Then it became a secret. Something to be mentioned only among us, if even that.

Passing

I have six sisters. Three are from my mother and father and are, like me, able to "pass." Of those, one chooses not to acknowledge any ancestry other than European. One acknowledges her other blood but considers herself white. The last one identifies herself as black and Hispanic, our mother being Venezuelan-Jamaican. Of my other three sisters, one is from my father and another woman before I was born; two are the children of my mother and another man, after my father died. All three are visibly mixed, with anything from Indian to Venezuelan to Chinese to British and African ancestry, but all three are still visibly black. I have six sisters. We all share parts of the same genetic codes.

Breaking the silence is not easy. There is no good way to tell someone you are black when you look white. If they are black, the worst scenario is that they will think you are putting them on or condescending to them or crazy or lying. If they are white, they will think you are crazy.

My aunt is Hispanic or white by U.S. standards of race, but she identifies herself as "Other" when she has to check the boxes. She says she is Jamaican. She is also a lesbian. When I am in college, I ask her what it's like to live as a lesbian, and she responds first that the word makes her uncomfortable. She prefers *gay*. It sounds less harsh. When she

The Challenges and Difficulties Encountered by Biracial Individuals

Biracial individuals are often susceptible to the following:

• Frequently experience some form of rejection from immediate and/or extended family members

• Anxiety regarding dual (or multiple) racial heritage

• Internal conflicts due to having parents from different racial/ethnic groups

• Problems choosing relationship partners due to racial complications

• May experience oppression as people of color and by people of color

• Tensions with one or more racial group based on ambiguous affiliation

• Pressure to identify with only one group based on physical characteristics

• Racial Dissonance: The inability to answer the question, "Who is my reference group?"

• Marginalization: A sense of feeling connected to both worlds but not a full member of either

"Facts Psychologists Know About Biracial Identity Formation," Mixed Folks Web site. www.mixedfolks.com.

---

meets people for the first time who don't know she is gay, she has to be careful, she says, and on guard for what they might say. Depending on the circumstances, she adds, she cannot be found out.

Tired of It All

I have lived in East Meredith for almost a year when this happens. Steve and I have moved from Maryland, outside of Washington, D.C., to a rural town in upstate New York. We live on a dirt road with cows half a mile away in any direction. I go to the post office two or three times a week, and John, the postmaster, knows me by name. Every time I come in, he chirps hello, smiles, and comments, "You've been busy." Today I tell him that two letters to home—one to my aunt, the other to my sister—have never reached them. He says it's not on this end but probably all those Hispanics and blacks in Miami who just take up space and don't do their jobs. I have known him for 11 months. Faced with his re-mark, I cannot find my voice. I leave in shame and stunned silence. We are moving to another small town in a few weeks, but to avoid seeing him again, I drive half an hour to the post office in the next town.

I tell this story to a militant "sistuh" I barely know be-cause she will see me as a coward and I need her censure. She does not disappoint, looks at me and sneers. "It is your re-sponsibility to speak and fight every time, *especially* since you can pass." I say nothing to her, either. I don't tell her of the time in Conyers, Ga., in that place where it is supposed to happen, where you go expecting to hear it, that I went against my friend's pleas, my friend who had taken me to her home town, and I stood up to a burly white man who said "nigger," who looked as if he would strike me down when I spoke back. I don't tell her that sometimes, it is also hard to admit, I am tired of it all.

No Habla Español

My grandmother considers herself white but also West Indian and maybe even British, England being the "mother country" from which she was adopted and brought to Trinidad to be raised. Most of all, she says, "I am human." My grandfather, by right if not biology, is her second husband, a Jamaican man who is also visibly mixed—his mother a light-skinned black woman, his father a Portuguese Jew. In Miami strangers auto-matically speak to him in Spanish, assuming he is Cuban. My grandmother delights in the looks on these strangers' faces when she, a white-skinned, blond-haired, blue-eyed woman—who lived in Venezuela for 12 years—answers in perfect Span-ish, *"El no habla español. Me ayuda?"*

Passing is the ability to go between or the inability to take root. Race is the desire to take root or the forcing to take root that which could otherwise go between.

Checking Boxes

Like my aunt, her sister—my mother—does not like the "boxes." She tells me that she checks whichever ones she is in the mood to check that day. Often, she says, she checks them all, "just to f— with them."

My mother has been a Rastafarian since she was 18 years old. She turned 46 this June. When I was growing up, I did not know it then, but I was learning that *white* meant Babylon, meant imperialism, economic privilege, racial and foreign domination, oppression. Whether she looks white or not, my mother says, she has fought against that type of whiteness her whole life. She has fought against and within her own skin.

Sometimes my skin feels as if it wants to burst into flames. Sometimes I wish it were a coat I could take off. Sometimes I look at it and see the proof of my life and my frequent, shameful desire to live outside of the body. Sometimes I look at it and see the proof of my life and my constant need to accept and live within this body. Sometimes I look at it and see one of my great-great-grandmothers, the mistress with whip in her hand. Sometimes through my aloe-colored eyes, I see another of my great-great-grandmothers, back arched against the curve of that lash.

"In relationship to the total number of biracial and multiracial people in this country, . . . products of mixed-race parentage are quite successful."

Having a Biracial Identity Is an Advantage

Raising Black and Biracial Children

In the following viewpoint the editors of *Raising Black and Biracial Children* claim that biracial children are more likely to be successful than are children of one race. For example, biracial children are able to move comfortably in more than one culture, the authors argue. Moreover, they maintain, biracial children often have conscientious, strong-willed, and assertive parents to motivate and support them. Ultimately, the authors conclude, the biracial child's biggest advantage is his or her ability to transcend racial categories.

As you read, consider the following questions:
1. What historical heroes do the authors cite as examples of multiracial success?
2. According to the authors, why do many people find the etymology of the word *mulatto* objectionable?
3. What is the biological analogy that suggests that mixed race children might be at an advantage, in the authors' view?

Raising Black and Biracial Children, "Are Biracial Children Successful?" October 31, 2001, p. 20. Reproduced by permission.

"All in all, they represent a rather successful group in this society." So said Dr. Alvin Poussaint in a 1985 article about biracial college students. R.C. Johnson, in an article on Asian/white biracial children in Hawaii, claims these children score very high on general knowledge IQ tests. Some studies suggest biracial adolescents have as high or higher self-esteem than single race adolescents. And the theory of hybrid vigor postulates that, through cross-gene pool breeding, biracial people are hardier and have greater genetic potential.

Multiracial Heroes

Great multiracial heroes like Frederick Douglass, W.E.B. Du Bois, Langston Hughes, Josephine Baker, James Audubon, Eartha Kitt, Lena Horne and recording artists Mariah Carey, Lenny Kravitz, and Sade certainly illustrate this success.

Most ethnic models and many ethnic actors are actually biracial or multiracial (Sonia Braga, Jennifer Beals, Naomi Campbell, Christy Turlington, etc.). And then there are athletes like golf great Tiger Woods, world decathlon champions, Daley Thompson and Dan O'Brien; skater Tai Babalonia, and Olympic gymnast Betty Okino. Numerous children in gifted and honors school programs are biracial.

It does seem, in relationship to the total number of biracial and multiracial people in this country, that products of mixed-race parentage are quite successful and often very beautiful.

Explaining the Success of Multiracial People

There are many possible explanations. Johnson's Hawaii research also documents that women who crossed racial/ethnic lines to marry (Asian/white) were more independent than women who marry within a racial/ethnic group. Considering the societal, professional and family pressures against interracial marriage, it's logical to suppose people who marry interracially are independent, strong willed and assertive. They are willing to buck the system for what they believe in. Surely these parents will raise self-willed, goal-oriented, independent children.

There is also research that shows interracially married partners tend to be better educated than people who marry within their racial/ethnic group. Clearly this means biracial children tend to grow up in educated families, and are expected to succeed in school.

Terry P. Wilson, in the book *Racially Mixed People in America*, discusses biracial Native American/white people who were able to use their biracial heritage to access both cultures. This gave them an advantage. On many occasions they could negotiate the needs of their tribal people with white land owners, businessmen and politicians. Sometimes they used this advantage to better themselves. But they were also able to help their own people. So much so that many tribes changed their definition of "full blood" to enable these mixed-race Indians to participate in tribal politics.

Wilson says, "Those who are comfortable half in the Indian world and half in the non-Indian world possess a third positive dimension stemming from biculturality that renders them 150% men."

Our children's access into two worlds, and the ability to feel comfortable in both, is a distinct advantage.

Conscientious Parents

And then there's the observation that interracial parents are very conscientious. They're more picky about the schools their children attend. They are always at the school demanding the best for their children. They are involved in PTAs, homework, field trips, etc. They know the rest of the world wants them to fail as parents. And—by God—they are going to prove the rest of the world wrong!

This position is supported by research results on Asian American children. These children are by far more academically successful than any other group of children, including white; research shows their parents have high expectations, know their children must work hard to overcome their background, and require lots of parent support. Parents of Asian American children spend a lot of time helping their children, monitoring the TV, and working with the school.

And these parents don't take a victim attitude: they believe that, with hard work, their children can succeed.

The research on black and biracial children adopted by white families shows that transracially adopted children have

171

as high, and sometimes higher, sense of ethnic pride and identity than do minority children raised in their biological homes, or in black adoptive homes. This suggests the effort and commitment made by the white parents does have a positive impact. It also implies that conscientious interracial parents will have a positive impact on their children.

Race Does Not Matter

For as long as I can remember, I have been constantly asked what problems I have, being biracial.

I have been asked this by television reporters, newspaper and magazine writers. Each time I have been lucky enough to answer that I have had no problems. It is very frustrating for me when everyone seems to expect me to have problems just because of my race. To me, race does not matter. If someone does not like me, I hope it is not because of my race, and I am not about to blame it on my race.

Maia Benjamin-Wardle, "Teentalk: Pointing Out Differences Simply Furthers the Stereotypes," Center for the Study of Biracial Children. www.csbc.cncfamily.com.

Interracial parents are very aware of the overall societal, professional and media biases against our families and children. We also know we must raise our children strong enough to withstand a history of negative writings, misguided scientific studies, and obnoxious characterizations of biracial people in movies, novels and dramas.

A Negative History

In a 1894 decision, a judge said, "the amalgamation of the races is not only unnatural, but is always productive of deplorable results . . . the offspring of these unnatural connections are generally sickly and effeminate, and they are inferior in physical development and strength, to the full blood of either race." Multiracial people were viewed as being weak physically, mentally, emotionally and morally, leading to early deaths and inability to reproduce, and eventually to group extinction (which is one reason many object to the word 'mulatto', because a mule cannot reproduce). They were characterized as depressive, criminal, chronically confused and ruled by passion.

Mixed-race women ("half-breed" Indians, Mexican mesti-zos, Eurasians and mulattos) were portrayed in books as sex-ually immoral, promiscuous, extremely passionate, and out of control.

Stonequist, a social scientist of the 1930's, called racial hy-brids the most obvious type of marginal man.

Australia and the United States of America were originally made up of criminals, social and religious misfits, slaves, in-dentured servants, and natives who civilized Europe viewed as primitive. These countries expended considerable individ-ual and collective energy to overcome this negative history, and have advanced beyond their European ancestors.

In striving to overcome a negative history, and to rise above the current societal pressure, interracial parents, bira-cial children and multiracial people will succeed. Almost ev-ery interracial family I have met in my travels across this country have been very conscious of the hurdles they must overcome, and very committed to raise successful children. This is the environmental argument.

Hybrid Vigor

And then there is the biological argument: hybrid vigor. Most successful plants and animals in today's highly special-ized agriculture are hybrids developed to increase yield and reduce vulnerability to diseases: Palomino and American Quarter horses, Brangus, Santa Gertruda and various Zebu cattle crosses, roses, tulips, trees, wheat, etc. The green rev-olution (dramatically increasing the yield of corn in develop-ing countries) is the direct result of a hybrid. Mixed-breed cattle were sent to Russia to replace the pure breed cows that cannot withstand the severe Russian winters.

The biological act of combining genes from two distinc-tive gene pools increases the health and strength of the re-sulting organism. With people it reduces the likelihood of genetically transmitted diseases and increases physical and mental possibilities.

And because interracial marriage maximizes these possi-bilities—both genotypically (the genes the person inherits) and phenotypically (the visual and physical result of those genes)—multiracial children will have new and different looks. This might explain the successes of multiracial fashion models and actors. The fashion world thrives on the novel, different and non-stereotypical images. Multiracial models are used a lot simply because they cannot be categorized as European, Asian, Hispanic, Native American or Black. And what's wrong with that?

When we consider our children are both the result of a caring, supportive and high expectation environment, and hybrid vigor, there is a temptation to claim they are, in fact, more successful and more beautiful than single race children. And for those of us (mostly parents) who are constantly told our children will fail this temptation is even greater.

Understandably, people like author Cynthia Nakashima, who in her article in *Racially Mixed People in America*, warn against this temptation. Part of her concern is that this position is based on the racist assumption that the white part of a biracial child's heritage is what makes them successful and beautiful, and the Asian part of a biracial person with Asian heritage makes them bright. Another reason is our memory of the tragic results of the Nazi concept of superior race.

While we obviously must reject this position of superiority, it's disheartening to realize many who express this concern are quite comfortable suggesting our children are intellectually, physically and socially inferior to single-race children, and that, for purely political reasons, any child with minority heritage must identify with their minority group. Surely, Hitler's insistence on a superior race was largely for political reasons.

We cannot afford to forget that the eugenics movement at the early part of the 20th century included multiracial people among those to be eliminated.

Defining Success

As Nakashima points out, when we talk about people being more or less successful than other people, we have to define what we mean by success. My definition of success is solving the fundamental problems of this country and the world. And one of these problems is racism.

According to this definition, maybe our children are more successful.

And, finally, there is the question of expectations. Asian American children are successful because their parents expect them to be. Most successful Americans have encountered someone in their lives—a parent, teacher, coach, Big Brother, etc.—who has had faith in their ability.

My wife always talks favorable of the Catholic high school teacher who believed she could become a writer.

One of the cruelest hoaxes being played on black children today is the black peer pressure against academically inclined black children, accusing them of trying to be white (some of these kids have even been beaten up). Other children, even white children, must handle equally restrictive expectations, from their own group and others. White kids are often told they can't dance, play certain music, or compete at certain sports. A biracial child can ignore all these limiting expectations.

A biracial child can be what he/she wants to be. And that's my idea of success!

"There is no definitive evidence that black foster or adoptive parents are better on average at raising black children than are white foster or adoptive parents."

Transracial Adoption Should Be Encouraged

Randall Kennedy

In the following viewpoint Randall Kennedy argues that race matching, the practice of requiring people to adopt children of the same race, shortchanges black children by denying them potentially loving homes. Whites can raise black children as effectively as black parents, Kennedy claims, and in fact can offer these children advantages. White parents, he maintains, can counter the psychological impact of racism and self-destructiveness. Kennedy, a professor at Harvard Law School, is author of *Interracial Intimacies*, from which the following viewpoint was excerpted.

As you read, consider the following questions:

1. What does Kennedy claim is the statistical rationale for allowing whites to adopt black children?
2. What analogy does the author make between raising a deaf child and raising a child of a different race?
3. According to Kennedy, is the experience of victimization an asset in parenting black children?

R ace matching is a destructive [adoption] practice in *all* its various guises, from moderate to extreme. It ought to be replaced by a system under which children in need of homes may be assigned to the care of foster or adoptive parents as quickly as reasonably possible, *regardless* of perceived racial differences. Such a policy would greatly benefit vulnerable children. It would also benefit American race relations.

First, consider the fact that at any given moment, hundreds of thousands of dependent children are bereft of parental protection, guidance, nurturance, and love. In the mid-1990s, more than half a million children lived in foster homes or institutions. This pool of parentless children is a tragic consequence of the personal catastrophes and social failures that kill parents, or maim them, or otherwise render them unfit to carry out their parental responsibilities. Among the gravest threats in this regard are disease, murder, child abuse, abandonment, drug addiction, imprisonment, and poverty. A disproportionately large percentage of parentless children are black. This is not a statistical accident; rather, it stems from a long and bitter history of slavery, segregation, and racially selective neglect and mistreatment. Disproportionately large numbers of blacks among the ranks of parentless children also reflect racial selectivity in the private preferences of those seeking to become foster or adoptive parents, the great majority of whom have a preference for children of the same race as themselves. This is especially so with respect to adoption. Because white adults dominate adoption markets both in numbers and in financial resources, their racial preferences have elevated the relative value of white children, who are, generally speaking, in higher demand than black children.

It is important to note that black adults do *not* lag in their willingness to adopt; indeed, relative to their share of the population, they are more likely to adopt than whites. In many locales, however, the pool of black parentless children overwhelms the available number of black prospective adoptive parents. In New York City in 1993, 75 percent of the children waiting for adoptive homes were African American, while blacks constituted only 21 percent of the city's population. In the mid-1990s, African American youngsters constituted 88 percent of the 40,000 children in the custody of the Cook County child-welfare authority, while only one third of the county's residents were African American. In such circumstances, even if their numbers increased considerably, black adopters alone would be unable to provide homes for all of the black children in need of parents.

A Shortage of Black Adoptive Parents

Some students of the subject assert that there is no real need for interracial adoption, as sufficient numbers of black adults would offer foster and adoptive homes to black children if only wrongful impediments could be removed. Even if black prospective foster and adoptive parents were being treated unfairly, the proper remedy would be to challenge the mistreatment directly, *not* to hold parentless children hostage in an attempt to force authorities to stop mistreating black prospective parents. Invidious discriminations against black prospective adoptive parents have certainly been carried out historically. But now that problem, though perhaps still active in certain places, is greatly diminished overall. Moreover, in many locales authorities make special efforts to recruit black foster and adoptive parents, even to the point of lowering or waiving general requirements.

Finally, even if there were a sufficient supply of prospective black foster and adoptive parents to accommodate all needy black youngsters, the question would remain: Is race matching a sound practice? For me, the answer is no. But before we consider the most difficult hypothetical case, let's return to the gritty reality of large numbers of children, disproportionately children of color, languishing in foster care or institutions as opposed to preferable adoptive settings. Race matching likely contributes to this problem. Anecdotal evidence suggests that in order to place children with adults deemed racially correct, social workers who strongly champion race matching will (at least temporarily) either decline to make a child eligible for adoption until a suitable black household can be found, or list only blacks on the roster of possible adoptive placements for the child. This strategy of racially aligning children and adults imposes a burden of delay, pushing back the moment at which a child becomes the primary responsibility of an adult who is willing to become his or her permanent parent. A delay of this kind is a cost in and of itself. In addition, it carries collateral consequences, insofar as it diminishes the chances that the child will *ever* be adopted. That is because for many adults, children become less attractive as potential adoptees as they age. What seems at first to be merely a brief wait may thus prevent certain youngsters from being adopted at all.

Race matching also hurts black potential adoptees by thinning the ranks of those who might adopt them. Whites who might otherwise have been happy to adopt regardless of racial differences may feel intimidated or stigmatized by race-matching policies and rhetoric. Any degree of race matching is a signal that authorities consider interracial adoption inferior to same-race adoption as a solution to a child's predicament. By treating interracial adoption as an unusually risky, deviant, or troubling endeavor, officials often signal that for them, it is at best only "better than nothing."

What Does the Research Show?

• The research that has been done to date suggests that transracial adoption is a viable means of providing stable homes for waiting children. Nearly a dozen studies consistently indicate that approximately 75% of transracially adopted preadolescent and younger children adjust well in their adoptive homes.

• In a 1995 study, transracial adoption was not found to be detrimental for the adoptee in terms of adjustment, self-esteem, academic achievement, peer relationships, parental and adult relationships.

"Transracial Adoption Statistics," Adoption.com. http://statistics.adoption. com.

By chasing away a substantial number of prospective adoptive parents, race-matching policies necessarily condemn some children to a childhood without any permanent parents whatsoever, or to a longer wait for adoption than they otherwise would have had to endure. A full understanding of the destructiveness of this unnecessary burden requires an assessment of institutional care and foster homes. Institutional care as it is currently configured typically offers parentless children a bleak existence. It is possible to imagine institutional settings in which stable, long-term, nurturing adult supervision could be provided to children in need. But in the United States, no such alternative is presently available. Instead, we have institutional settings in which no single adult is cloaked with even the temporary mantle of "parent," and in which children are thus deprived of every benefit of having in their corner an adult whose primary responsibility, twenty-four hours a day, is the well-being of his or her charges. Many institutional homes are, moreover, beset by a wide array of interrelated difficulties: insufficient pay for staff, poorly trained and unmotivated employees, and high turnover of personnel. . . .

Racial Discrimination

The strongest argument against race matching . . . is that it inhibits or even prevents the progress of parentless children toward adoption—the alternative that would give them their best chance of a long-term, secure family attachment. But other arguments can also be made against the practice. First off, insofar as race matching is a form of racial discrimination, it bears a burden of justification that cannot be sustained. Proponents of race matching have frequently been able to shift onto their antagonists the burden of persuasion, but this is precisely the opposite of what should be its proper allocation. Those who wish to engage in racial selectivity should be called upon to justify *their* position, given that racial discrimination is presumptively wrong. Federal and state statutory and constitutional law generally either forbids such discrimination absolutely or allows it only exceptionally, when those who seek to discriminate can offer a compelling justification. In the interracial-adoption controversy, the onus of persuasion has illogically fallen on those who desire to *remove* racial considerations as a routine factor in child-placement decision making. By rights, proponents of race matching should have to defend the racial discrimination they embrace. And before they can be permitted to differentiate racially among prospective adoptive parents, supporters of race matching should have to make a case—a strong case—for their approach. It is the race matcher, in other words, who should bear the burden—the heavy burden—of justifying what American law presumptively prohibits: judging people, even if only in part, on the basis of their apparent racial background.

As we have noted, one oft-cited rationale for favoring same-race placements for black children is that African American parents can typically better equip African American youngsters with the tools they will need if they are to survive and prosper in a racist society dominated by whites. . . .

Those who confidently assert . . . that black adults are better able than whites to parent black children rely on the hunch that as inevitable victims of antiblack racism themselves, black adults will be more capable of teaching their charges how to face and overcome that racism. This is not, however, a proper basis for racial selectivity. . . . There is no definitive evidence that black foster or adoptive parents are better on average at raising black children than are white foster or adoptive parents. Many people simply take this on faith, as a matter of "common sense." But common sense is often tainted by baleful habits of thought and can be highly resistant to unexpected realities.

What White Parents Can Offer Black Children

Those who propound the "survival skills" justification typically slight any possibility that white parents may have valuable knowledge of their own to impart to black youngsters on the subject of prejudice, racial and otherwise. As Professor Kim Forde-Mazrui has pointed out,

> white people, as individuals, have not been spared maltreatment from others, and white parents routinely teach their children how to cope with insults from others. . . . [A white person] called "commie" for protesting [against the Vietnam war] or a woman referred to as "girl" by her boss has some experience from which to empathize with her Black child who is called "nigger" at school. A person who stutters, limps, or cannot hear well also gains analogous experience that could benefit a Black child.

Some might argue that racism is more pervasive and debilitating than the types of prejudice alluded to by Forde-Mazrui. Even if that is so, however, why should we not assume that here, as in other areas, parents will endeavor to familiarize themselves with and master the challenges faced by their children? We presume that parents who are initially ignorant as to deafness or genius will educate themselves if they have a deaf or intellectually advanced child. Similarly, we should presume that parents who know nothing of the realities of being black in America will learn what they can about antiblack racism and related challenges.

Whites, moreover, might be able to bring to bear on behalf of their black children advantages generally denied to blacks. They might be able to share knowledge gleaned from their experience on the white side of the racial divide. As for forestalling the crippling psychological complexes that racism often insidiously fosters within the minds of African Americans, Professor Forde-Mazrui has shrewdly remarked that a message of racial equality voiced by a white parent may, to a child, have greater credibility than the same message offered up by a black parent, inasmuch as the black parent could be perceived as having a more self-interested stake in refuting claims of white superiority. In Forde-Mazrui's words, "A white parent's denial of Black inferiority may be more believable because it is less self-serving."

Survival Skills

Another weakness of the race marchers' "survival skills" justification derives from their romanticization of the heuristic value of simply being a victim. Victimization *may* teach a person valuable lessons that he or she will be able to pass on to others, or it may not. People of all kinds frequently fail to learn from or impart to others the available lessons embedded in various experiences. The experience of victimization is only a *potential* asset; a person must do something with it before it can become an *actual* asset. Moreover, if victimization can be a source of useful knowledge, it can also be a source of destructive myopia. It is certainly true that many African Americans have passed down to their progeny wise counsel proofed in the crucible of racial injustice. But the champions of race matching typically suggest that the burdens imposed on black adults by white racism are *invariably* met by responses that are both self-protective and socially beneficial—the sort of responses, that is, that *should* be held up for emulation. Unfortunately, the truth is that racism can also cripple its victims and, worse, result in the development of adaptive behaviors that may lead those victims to hobble their own children. Cruelly frustrated by racial bars that have now been lowered, some blacks discourage their offspring from pursuing certain educational or occupational ambitions though such aims are now attainable. Some African Americans have so internalized Negrophobic attitudes that they themselves harbor anti-black racial prejudices. Much of the energy of the civil rights and Black Power movements was aimed at undoing the cycles of self-limitation, self-contempt, and self-destruction set in motion by a cruelly oppressive social order dominated by white racism. Despite the best efforts of those movements, however, black self-destructiveness persists and must be taken into account in any serious assessment of the internal racial dynamics of black communities. In sum, African American victims of racial oppression take away from their experiences all kinds of lessons. Some victims acquire and pass on commendable beliefs. Others assimilate and perpetuate pernicious notions such as the idea that "Niggers ain't shit."

An American Problem

Mention of social pathology in black communities often triggers yet another spate of attacks on interracial adoption. One charge is that such adoptions denigrate African American communities by implying that blacks are unable to care for "their own." Another complaint is that some defenses of interracial adoption are predicated on the belief that black adults have little of worth to offer black children. In response, three points are important to voice. First, it is probably true that some defenders of interracial adoption embrace racist stereotypes about blacks, including the derogatory notion that African Americans are generally incompetent when it comes to building strong families. The mere existence of such attitudes, however, in no way invalidates the conclusion that interracial adoptions should be freely permitted. People do sometimes favor good policies for bad reasons. Racism, after all, animated a substantial number of anti-slavery whites who opposed Negro bondage precisely because it entailed the presence of blacks.

Second, responsibility for addressing the plight of parentless children in America should not be allocated along racial lines, with African American adoptees being designated as the special province of blacks, Euro-American adoptees as that of whites, and so on. The plight of African American children should be deemed an *American* problem, to be dealt with by the whole of American society. Concomitantly, the unmet needs of these children should be seen as reflecting badly not on any discrete racial group—blacks—but on American society in its entirety. That there exist so many parentless children in terrible circumstances, a disproportionate number of whom are black, is not an Afro-American disgrace but an American disgrace.

Third, there are things more important than the perceived image problems arising from transracial adoption. Expeditiously placing children in secure homes should be a higher priority than assuaging hurt racial pride.

"The [transracial] adoption industry forcibly removes children of color from their families and communities and assimilates them into their new white families and society."

Transracial Adoption Should Be Discouraged

Stephanie Cho and Kim So Yung

In the following viewpoint Stephanie Cho and Kim So Yung, transracial adoptees who identify themselves as transracial abductees, describe the racism they experienced while growing up. According to the authors, not only did their parents describe them in racist terms, such as China dolls, their parents would punish them for identifying the racism they experienced in the community. Moreover, they argue, transracial adoptees are often prevented from exploring their own culture. Cho and Yung founded Transracial Abductees, an organization that helps transracial adoptees integrate into communities of color.

As you read, consider the following questions:

1. What sort of racism did the authors encounter growing up?
2. How did Yung's parents react to her "coming out" as a person of color?
3. Why, according to Cho and Yung, do many whites choose to adopt children of color?

Stephanie Cho and Kim So Yung, "Abductees Speak: Transracial Adoptees Take on the Adoption Agencies," *Eurasian Nation*, June 2003. Copyright © 2003 by Stephanie Cho and Kim So Yung. Reproduced by permission.

S tephanie Cho and Kim So Yung are co-founders of Trans-racial Abductees, an organization that works to educate transracial adoptees and communities of color and expose the unequal power between the white adoption industry and children of color adoptees. They choose the word "abduction" to describe how the adoption industry forcibly removes children of color from their families and communities and assimilates them into their new white families and society.

In this article, they reflect on their experiences growing up in the Northwest United States, when they started thinking about racism and adoption, and how they became political about it.

Stephanie: Sometimes my memories are pictures that are revisited. I can't remember if it is a picture I saw when I was younger or if it is really my own memory but I think I first noticed racism when I met my white family. There have been arguments made that racism happens when contact between white and colored meet. This might have been true for me.

"China Doll"

When I first came here, my mom used to say I was so small I looked like a "china doll". She meant that as a term of endearment but I would describe it now as racism.

Knowing that I was adopted and recognizing racism happened at the same time for me. People acknowledging the fact that I was adopted was also acknowledging that I was a person of color. This would usually result in someone saying I looked like a "china doll" or saying something about my imported status, like when did you get her like I was just shipped and delivered onsite (which I was).

I started becoming political when I came out as queer. Queer people are all about identity issues and from that I re-identified and basically reclaimed me back. I used to work on people of color issues without really working on transracial adoption issues. Like my assimilation taught me, transracial adoption is not a people of color issue. I know now, centrally, my adoption is one of the major reasons I organize around people of color issues and that even my queer identity is centered around my transracial adoption identity. I know other adoptees that work in the people of color movement but don't work in the transracial abductee movement. I think that will start to change in the next 5–10 years, but for now it is a matter of doing some strong political education with other people of color organizations. They need to learn to be good allies of transracial adoptees that work in their movement and learn to support them as a moving force in the people of color movement because transracial adoption is a people of color issue.

A Certain Sting

So Yung: I always knew I was adopted because of the obvious difference in looks between my white adoptive parents and me. My parents always tried to downplay it, and teach me that I was no different from anyone else, meaning that I was "as good as white." All the time I was growing up, I wasn't allowed to question my parents' definition of what my being a Korean adoptee meant. I wasn't allowed to explore Korean culture or ask questions about the war in Korea. I especially wasn't allowed to talk about racism.

I always felt a certain sting when my family or people we met would say something racist. They would talk about how beautiful and exotic I was. My mom would always coo over my "rosebud lips." My friends would express jealousy over my "silky straight hair" and "smooth, clear skin." They would always want my hair and acne-free skin, but never my skin color or my "Chinese" eyes.

When I was around middle school age I began to name the racism I felt happening. That was quickly squashed by my parents, who used physical punishment to keep my brother, also a Korean adoptee, and me from "accusing" people of racism. During that brief period of rebellion, my brother and I actually talked about how people in our family, school, and whole town were racist, and would make a point of calling each other by our Korean names. But we were totally dependent on our parents. We were very isolated in a small, white town. Everything around us taught us that we shouldn't criticize our parents; they weren't open to having their views and choices questioned. I became really focused on school and grades. I lived in my head a lot, reading constantly and being a perfect student. Looking back, it seems like I turned the part of me that was critical off. I had to wait until it was safer to have those kinds of thoughts.

A Last Resort

As I was growing up, my parents told me different things about my heritage—I was Ethiopian, Mexican, black, white. But today, if someone asks me to describe myself, I say without hesitation that I am a 25-year-old African American woman. Coming to that conclusion was part of a long internal struggle about who I am, and where I came from—a struggle that has everything to do with my childhood in a white family. . . .

It is too easy to say I am against transracial adoption. But I do think it should be a last resort. Although love should be enough, love does not prepare an African American child for the society we live in. And love does not replace the importance of knowing your own ethnicity and culture.

Rachel Noerdlinger, *Washington Post*.

It was when I had been living away from my parents for about two years, and had started to organize against racism at the university I was attending, that I began exploring those questions I had about racism and transracial adoption again. I think it took organizing around more general people of color issues for me to realize the political impact of coming out as a transracial adoptee to other people of color, and as a person of color to my adoptive family. That may sound strange, but it's exactly what I mean. I tried to assert myself as a person of color with a person of color consciousness to my white family, and to this day I don't think any of them really gets it; they still reassure me that I'm 'just like their real daughter,' and that they don't see a difference "whether someone's black, red, green, or purple."

Trying to politicize the transracial adoption issue in general is a similar struggle. People aren't used to thinking of transracial adoptees as people of color, and really haven't been taught to view transracial adoption as a political issue. There's a lot of wrong information and stereotypes about transracial adoptees out there. We're especially interested in reframing transracial adoption as an issue that affects all communities of color. That's going to involve breaking down some of the barriers that transracial adoption sets up between adoptees and other people of color.

Our Vision for Transracial Abductees

We like that Transracial Abductees is an activist organization made up of transracial adoptees who are angry and critical and will continue to push people's thinking about transracial adoption and people of color issues in general. Stephanie is a paid community organizer working on low-income issues and thinks it is a great job, but the issues are mainstreamed liberal issues. Transracial Abductees, on the other hand, can be more outspoken and direct about our views on the adoption industry.

We envision the organization as an outlet and movement starting organization that mostly focuses on political education for the time being and later organizes transracial adoptees on local, national, and international legislation and has deprogramming camps all over the world.

Building a Transracial Abductee Movement

There are rumblings of a transracial abductee movement just beginning to surface. The very structure of transracial adoption is based on assimilating to white American society, and mainstream transracial and international adoptee organizations continue to exist within this structure. Many adoptees are isolated from communities of color. To organize and pretty much reverse that assimilation process is a serious battle. Also, because racism has changed and evolved into new and more sophisticated forms, this has had major impact on the white people who choose to adopt children of color. Now, transracial adoption is viewed as the ultimate form of cultural competency that puts whites on the road to becoming worldly anti-racist people. Many choose to adopt children of color, not just because of the "save the needy" aspect, but for their own social gain and legitimacy in the world of people of color.

A movement around transracial adoption that is critical of the adoption industry is beginning to shape itself in really creative ways. Our website is one example and there are numerous groups forming in bigger cities.

In 5 years, we would like to see that the transracial abductee movement has become a movement and that there
are many transracial adoptees actively organizing in their
communities.

In 10 years, there will probably be a mainstream organization that works on transracial adoptee/abductee issues that
is centralized in a major city. Hopefully, there will be a fac-
tion of the organization that stays pretty angry and more
militant. In ten years, the isolated pockets of abductees that
exist now will be much more connected and will really be
able to mobilize adoptees on a larger scale.

Periodical Bibliography

The following articles have been selected to supplement the diverse views presented in this chapter.

Fred A. Bernstein	"Married or Not, It's a Full House," *New York Times*, November 20, 2003.
Courtney Edelhart	"One Family, Two Worlds," *Indianapolis Star*, December 6, 2004.
Audrey Edwards	"Bring Me Home a Black Girl," *Essence*, November 2002.
Adam Goodheart	"Change of Heart," *AARP Magazine*, May/June 2004.
Emilie Hammerstein	"Sticky Rice for Yom Kippur," *Eurasian Nation*, November 2002.
Andrew Herrmann	"Mixed-Race Marriages—and Tolerance—Soar," *Chicago SunTimes*, July 24, 2005.
John Kenyon	"Two Notes on Being in an Interracial Marriage," *Multiracial Activist* (www.multiracial.com), May/June 2004.
Carmen Van Kerckhove	"Biracial Asians Break from Family Tradition," *Multiracial Activist* (www.multiracial.com), August/September 2002.
Andrew Murr	"Dating the White Way," *Newsweek*, August 9, 2005.
Eleanor Stacy Parker	"He Loves Me, He Loves Me Not," *Salon*, February 17, 2000.
Sheila M. Poole	"Canadians Look South to Adopt Black Kids," *Atlanta Journal-Constitution*, August 24, 2004.
Sam Sasso	"Guess Who's Coming to Dinner?" *Urban Mozaik*, May 2001.
Louis Whitehead	"Denying Assistance to Mixed Bloods Perpetuates Genocide," *IMDiversity.com*, 2005. www.imdiversity.com/villages/native/history_heritage/whitehead_mixedbloods_genocide.asp.
Mary Wiltenburg and Amanda Paulson	"All in the (Mixed-Race) Family: A U.S. Trend," *Christian Science Monitor*, August 28, 2003.

For Further Discussion

Chapter 1

1. Compare Ward Connerly's and Emil Guillermo's approach to racial classification. Which approach do you think would serve people of all races best? Explain, citing from the text.

2. Eve Brown uses her personal experience as a starting point to talk about the drawbacks of racial classifications. Do you think this makes her argument stronger or weaker? Explain, citing from the viewpoint.

3. Roger Kimball claims that "one of America's greatest achievements is having eliminated the racial and ethnic components that historically were central to its identity." What evidence does he cite to support this claim? Is it convincing? Why or why not?

4. bell hooks argues for the advantages of racial segregation. What examples does she provide to support her claim? Do you agree, or do you think all forms of segregation should be discouraged? Explain.

Chapter 2

1. William Norman Grigg maintains that emigration from Mexico poses a terrorist threat to the United States. What evidence does he provide to support his views? Is this evidence persuasive? Explain, citing from his viewpoint.

2. The League of United Latin American Citizens and Mexican American Legal Defense and Educational Fund asserts that it is essential to take history into account in talking about Mexican immigration to the United States. To what extent do you think the history of the two countries is important in addressing this issue? Explain, citing from the text.

3. *Rethinking Schools* contends that bilingual education is a human right. Samuel Huntington opposes bilingual education because he believes that it threatens American culture. Both authors appear to be discussing different values. Which values do you consider more important? Does this influence which viewpoint you find more persuasive? Explain, citing from the viewpoints.

Chapter 3

1. Clarence Thomas contends that affirmative action hurts those it intends to help. What evidence does he use to justify his claim? Is this reason enough to oppose affirmative action? Explain.

2. Mitchell J. Chang and Peter Wood agree that having a diverse student population alone is not sufficient to promote diversity.

Chang, however, believes that diversity can improve education while Wood claims that it does not. What evidence does each author provide to support his view? What similarities do you see in the evidence each provides? What differences? Explain your answers, citing from the text.

3. Walter Benn Michaels claims that race-based affirmative action leads to a very narrow form of diversity, one that does not take into account cultural and socioeconomic differences. What evidence does Michaels provide that this is the case? What assumptions about the goal of affirmative action underlie his conclusions?

Chapter 4

1. According to Lakshmi Chaudhry, what are some of the stereotypes that arise with interracial dating? Does she offer convincing evidence in her viewpoint that her solution—dating within one's own race or culture—is the superior one? Why or why not?

2. Shara McCallum describes her encounter with a bigoted postal worker. What reasons does she give for responding the way she does? Do you think these reasons justify her response? Why or why not?

3. Stephanie Cho and Kim So Yung imply that racial and cultural barriers are often insurmountable. Is their evidence, based on your personal experience, convincing? Why or why not?

Organizations to Contact

American Civil Liberties Union (ACLU)
125 Broad St., Eighteenth Floor, New York, NY 10004
(212) 549-2500 • fax: (212) 549-2646
Web site: www.aclu.org

The ACLU is a national organization that works to defend Americans' civil rights as guaranteed by the U.S. Constitution. The ACLU publishes and distributes policy statements, pamphlets, and the semiannual newsletter *Civil Liberties Alert*.

Amnesty International (AI)
322 Eighth Ave., New York, NY 10004-2400
(212) 807-8400 • (800) AMNESTY (266-3789)
fax: (212) 627-1451
Web site: www.amnesty-usa.org

Amnesty International is a grassroots activist organization that works to end and prevent human rights abuses, including freedom of conscience and expression and freedom from discrimination. The *Amnesty International Report* is published annually. Reports are available by mail and on its Web site.

Anti-Defamation League (ADL)
823 United Nations Plaza, New York, NY 10017
(212) 490-2525
Web site: www.adl.org

ADL works to stop the defamation of Jews and to ensure fair treatment for all U.S. citizens. It publishes the periodic *ADL Law Report* and *Law Enforcement Bulletin* as well as other reports.

Cato Institute
1000 Massachusetts Ave. NW, Washington, DC 20001-5403
(202) 842-0200 • fax: (202) 842-3490
e-mail: cato@cato.org • Web site: www.cato.org

The Cato Institute is a libertarian public policy research foundation dedicated to limiting the role of government and protecting individual liberties. It researches claims of discrimination and opposes affirmative action. The institute offers numerous publications, including the *Cato Journal*, the bimonthly newsletter *Cato Policy Report*, and the quarterly magazine *Regulation*.

Center for the Study of Popular Culture (CSPC)
9911 W. Pico Blvd., Suite 1290, Los Angeles, CA 90035
(310) 843-3699 • fax: (310) 843-3692
Web site: www.cspc.org

CSPC is a conservative educational organization that addresses topics such as political correctness, cultural diversity, and discrimination. Its civil rights project promotes equal opportunity for all individuals and provides legal assistance to citizens challenging affirmative action. The center publishes four magazines: *Heterodoxy*, *Defender*, *Report Card*, and *COMINT*.

Citizens' Commission on Civil Rights (CCCR)
2000 M St. NW, Suite 400, Washington, DC 20036
(202) 659-5565 • fax: (202) 223-5302
e-mail: citizens@cccr.org • Web site: www.cccr.org

CCCR monitors the federal government's enforcement of antidiscrimination laws and promotes equal opportunity for all. It publishes reports on affirmative action and desegregation as well as the book *One Nation Indivisible: The Civil Rights Challenge for the 1990s*.

Heritage Foundation
214 Massachusetts Ave. NE, Washington, DC 20002-4999
(202) 546-4400 • fax: (202) 546-8328
e-mail: info@heritage.org • Web site: www.heritage.org

The foundation is a conservative public policy research institute that advocates freemarket principles, individual liberty, and limited government. It believes the private sector, not government, should be relied upon to ease social problems and to improve the status of minorities. The Heritage Foundation publishes the quarterly *Policy Review* and the bimonthly newsletter *Heritage Today* as well as numerous monographs, books, and papers.

National Association for the Advancement of Colored People (NAACP)
1156 Fifteenth St. NW, Suite 915, Washington, DC 20005
(202) 463-2940 • fax: (202) 463-2953
Web site: www.naacp.org

The NAACP is the oldest and largest civil rights organization in the United States. Its principal objective is to ensure the political, educational, social, and economic equality of minorities. It publishes the magazine *Crisis* ten times a year as well as a variety of newsletters, books, and pamphlets.

National Network for Immigrant and Refugee Rights (NNIRR)
310 Eighth St., Suite 307, Oakland, CA 94607
(510) 465-1984 • fax: (510) 465-1885
e-mail: nnirr@nnirr.org • Web site: www.nnirr.org

The network includes community, church, labor, and legal groups committed to the cause of equal rights for all immigrants. These groups work to end discrimination and unfair treatment of illegal immigrants and refugees. It publishes a monthly newsletter, *Network News.*

National Urban League
120 Wall St., Eighth Floor, New York, NY 10005
(212) 558-5300 • fax: (212) 344-5332
Web site: www.nul.org

A community service agency, the National Urban League aims to eliminate institutional racism in the United States. It also provides services for minorities who experience discrimination in employment, housing, welfare, and other areas. It publishes the report *The Price: A Study of the Costs of Racism in America* and the annual *State of Black America.*

Poverty and Race Research Action Council (PRRAC)
3000 Connecticut Ave. NW, Suite 200, Washington, DC 20008
(202) 387-9887 • fax: (202) 387-0764
e-mail: info@prrac.org • Web site: www.prrac.org

The Poverty and Race Research Action Council is a nonpartisan, national, not-for-profit organization convened by major civil rights, civil liberties, and antipoverty groups. PRRAC's purpose is to link social science research to advocacy work in order to successfully address problems at the intersection of race and poverty. Its bimonthly publication, *Poverty and Race,* often includes articles on race- and income-based inequities in the United States.

The Prejudice Institute
Stephens Hall Annex, TSU, Towson, MD 21204-7097
(410) 830-2435 • fax: (410) 830-2455
Web site: www.prejudiceinstitute.org

The Prejudice Institute is a national research center concerned with violence and intimidation motivated by prejudice. It conducts research, supplies information on model programs and legislation, and provides education and training to combat prejudicial violence. The Prejudice Institute publishes research reports, bibliographies, and the quarterly newsletter *Forum.*

United States Commission on Civil Rights
624 Ninth St. NW, Suite 500, Washington, DC 20425
(202) 376-7533 • Publications: (202) 376-8128
Web site: www.usccr.gov

A fact-finding body, the commission reports directly to Congress and the president on the effectiveness of equal opportunity laws and programs. A catalog of its numerous publications can be obtained from its Publication Management Division.

Bibliography of Books

Richard D. Alba — *Remaking the American Mainstream: Assimilation and Contemporary Immigration.* Cambridge, MA: Harvard University Press, 2003.

Derrick A. Bell — *Silent Covenants:* Brown v. Board of Education *and the Unfulfilled Hopes for Racial Reform.* New York: Oxford University Press, 2004.

Emily Bernard, ed. — *Some of My Best Friends.* New York: HarperCollins, 2005.

Erica Chito Childs — *Navigating Interracial Borders: Black-White Couples and Their Social Worlds.* New Brunswick, NJ: Rutgers University Press, 2005.

Amy Coughlin — *Cross-Cultural Adoption: How to Answer Questions from Family, Friends, and Community.* Washington, DC: LifeLine, 2004.

Michael Eric Dyson — *The Michael Eric Dyson Reader.* New York: Basic Civitas, 2004.

Henry Louis Gates Jr. — *Behind the Color Line: Dialogues with African Americans.* New York: Warner, 2004.

Elzbieta M. Gozdarziak — *Beyond the Gateway: Immigrants in a Changing America.* Lanham, MD: Lexington, 2005.

Joseph L. Graves Jr. — *The Race Myth.* New York: Penguin, 2004.

Lani Guinier — *Who's Qualified?* Boston: Beacon: 2001.

Patricia Gurin et al. — *Defending Diversity: Affirmative Action at the University of Michigan.* Ann Arbor: University of Michigan Press, 2004.

Victor David Hanson — *Mexifornia: A State of Becoming.* San Francisco: Encounter, 2003.

Dorothy Hoobler — *We Are Americans: Voices of the Immigrant Experience.* New York: Scholastic Reference, 2003.

Jesse L. Jackson — *The Case for Affirmative Action in University Admissions.* Berkeley, CA: Bay Tree, 2005.

Gerald David Jaynes — *Immigration and Race: New Challenges for American Democracy.* New Haven, CT: Yale University Press, 2000.

Ira Katznelson — *When Affirmative Action Was White: An Untold History of Racial Inequality in Twentieth-Century America.* New York: W.W. Norton, 2005.

Desmond King — *Making Americans: Immigration, Race, and the Origins of the Diverse Democracy.* Cambridge, MA: Harvard University Press, 2000.

Ruben Martinez	*The New Americans.* New York: The New Press, 2004.
John McWhorter	*Authentically Black: Essays for the Black Silent Majority.* New York: Gotham, 2004.
Barack Obama	*Dreams from My Father: A Story of Race and Inheritance.* New York: Three Rivers, 2004.
Claudine Chiawei O'Hearn, ed.	*Half and Half: Writers on Growing Up Biracial and Bicultural.* New York: Pantheon, 1998.
Jorge Ramos	*Dying to Cross: The Worst Immigrant Tragedy in American History.* New York: Rayo, 2005.
Richard Rodriguez	*Brown: The Last Discovery of America.* New York: Penguin, 2003.
Barbara Katz Rothman	*Weaving a Family: Untangling Race and Adoption.* Boston: Beacon, 2005.
Sharon Rush	*Loving Across the Color Line: A White Adoptive Mother Learns About Race.* Lanham, MD: Rowman & Littlefield, 2000.
Greg Stohr	*A Black and White Case: How Affirmative Action Survived Its Greatest Legal Challenge.* Princeton, NJ: Bloomberg, 2004.
Tim J. Wise	*Affirmative Action: Racial Preferences in Black and White.* New York: Routledge, 2005.
Victor Zuniga and Ruben Hernandez-Leon	*New Destinations: Mexican Immigration in the U.S.* New York: Russell Sage Foundation, 2005.

Index

201